THE GREAT COOKS' GUIDE TO

Soups

GREAT COOKS' LIBRARY

Appetizers
Breads
Cakes
Chickens, Ducks & Other Poultry
Children's Cookery
Clay Cookery
Cookies
Crêpes & Soufflés
Fish Cookery
Flambéing Desserts
Ice Cream & Other Frozen Desserts
Omelets from Around the World
Pasta & Noodle Dishes
Pies & Tarts
Rice Cookery
Salads
Soups
Vegetable Cookery
Wine Drinks
Woks, Steamers & Fire Pots

America's leading food authorities share their home-tested
recipes and expertise on cooking equipment and techniques

THE GREAT COOKS' GUIDE TO

Soups

A BEARD GLASER WOLF BOOK

RANDOM HOUSE, NEW YORK

Front Cover (left to right, top to bottom): Iowa Corn Chowder, page 38; California Cioppino, page 9 *(copper casserole courtesy Charles F. Lamalle)*.

Back Cover (left to right, top to bottom): *(stainless-steel chinois and stockpot courtesy The Professional Kitchen);* Cream of Carrot Soup, page 40 *(soup bowl and plate courtesy Groundworks);* French Onion Soup, page 37.

Interior Photographs: Page 5, *chinois courtesy The Professional Kitchen, food mill courtesy Charles F. Lamalle;* Page 6 (top), *stockpot courtesy The Professional Kitchen.*

Book Design by Milton Glaser, Inc.

Cover Photograph by Richard Jeffery

Food Styling by Lucy Wing
Props selected by Yvonne McHarg and Beard Glaser Wolf Ltd.

Library of Congress Cataloguing in Publication Data
Main entry under title:

The Great Cooks' Guide to Soups.
(The Great Cooks' Library)
1. Soups.   I. Series.
TX757.G73   641.8'13   77-90241
ISBN: 0-394-73608-7

Manufactured in the United States of America
2 4 6 8 9 7 5 3

We have gathered together some of the great cooks in this country to share their recipes—and their expertise—with you. As you read the recipes, you will find that in certain cases techniques will vary. This is as it should be: Cooking is a highly individual art, and our experts have arrived at their own personal methods through years of experience in the kitchen.

THE EDITORS

SENIOR EDITORS

Wendy Afton Rieder
Kate Slate

ASSOCIATE EDITORS

Lois Bloom
Susan Lipke

EDITORIAL ASSISTANT

Christopher Carter

PRODUCTION MANAGER

Emily Aronson

EDITORIAL STAFF

Mardee Haidin
Michael Sears
Patricia Thomas

CONTRIBUTORS

Introduction by Emanuel and Madeline Greenberg

Eliza and Joshua Baer have worked in various phases of the restaurant business on the West Coast and are currently planning a cookbook.

Michael Batterberry, author of several books on food, art and social history, is also a painter, and is editor and food critic for a number of national magazines. He has taught at James Beard's cooking classes in New York and many of his original recipes have appeared in *House & Garden, House Beautiful* and *Harper's Bazaar.*

Elizabeth Schneider Colchie is a noted food consultant who has done extensive recipe development and testing as well as research into the history of foods and cookery. She was on the editorial staff of *The Cooks' Catalogue* and *The International Cooks' Catalogue* amd has written numerous articles for such magazines as *Gourmet, House & Garden* and *Family Circle.*

Carol Cutler, who has been a food columnist for the *Washington Post,* is a graduate of the Cordon Bleu and L'Ecole des Trois Gourmands in Paris. She is the author of *Haute Cuisine for Your Heart's Delight* and *The Six-Minute Soufflé and Other Culinary Delights.* She has also written for *House & Garden, American Home* and *Harper's Bazaar.*

Rona Deme, a native of England, ran a pork store with her husband for 25 years and in 1972 opened up The Country Host, a gourmet food shop in New York City.

Florence Fabricant is a freelance writer, reporting on restaurants and food for *The New York Times*, *New York* magazine and other publications. She was on the staff of *The Cooks' Catalogue* and editor of the paperback edition. She also contributed to *The International Cooks' Catalogue* and *Where to Eat in America*.

Emanuel and Madeline Greenberg co-authored *Whiskey in the Kitchen* and are consultants to the food and beverage industry. Emanuel, a home economist, is a regular contributor to the food columns of *Playboy* magazine. Both contribute to *House Beautiful, Harper's Bazaar* and *Travel & Leisure*.

Nan Mabon, a freelance food writer and cooking teacher in New York City, is also the cook for a private executive dining room on Wall Street. She studied at the Cordon Bleu school in London.

Gloria Bley Miller is the author of *Learn Chinese Cooking in Your Own Kitchen* and *The Thousand Recipe Chinese Cookbook*.

Maurice Moore-Betty, owner-operator of The Civilized Art Cooking School, food consultant and restaurateur, is author of *Cooking for Occasions, The Maurice Moore-Betty Cooking School Book of Fine Cooking* and *The Civilized Art of Salad Making*.

Jane Moulton, a food writer for the *Plain Dealer* in Cleveland, took her degree in foods and nutrition. As well as reporting on culinary matters and reviewing food-related books for the *Plain Dealer*, she has worked in recipe development, public relations and catering.

Paul Rubinstein is the author of *Feasts for Two, The Night Before Cookbook* and *Feasts for Twelve (or More)*. He is a stockbroker and the son of pianist Artur Rubinstein.

Maria Luisa Scott and Jack Denton Scott co-authored the popular *Complete Book of Pasta* and have also written many other books on food, including *Informal Dinners for Easy Entertaining, Mastering Microwave Cooking, The Best of the Pacific Cookbook,* and *Cook Like a Peasant, Eat Like a King.* With the renowned chef Antoine Gilly, they wrote *Feast of France*.

Satish Sehgal is the founder of the successful Indian Oven restaurant in New York City, which specializes in northern Indian cuisine. He began developing recipes for northern specialties while an engineering student in southern India and later abandoned engineering for the food world.

Ruth Spear is the author of *The East Hampton Cookbook* and writes occasional pieces on food for *New York* magazine. She is currently at work on a new cookbook.

Paula Wolfert, author of *Mediterranean Cooking* and *Couscous and Other Good Food from Morocco*, is also a cooking teacher and consultant. She has written articles for *Vogue* and other magazines.

Nicola Zanghi is the owner-chef of Restaurant Zanghi in Glen Cove, New York. He started his apprenticeship under his father at the age of thirteen, and is a graduate of two culinary colleges. He has been an instructor at the Cordon Bleu school in New York City.

Contents

VEGETABLE SOUPS

SAVORY AND SWEET COLD SOUPS

Soups

An 18th-century sage opined that "of soup and love, the first is best." *Not necessarily*, but if made right, soup, too, can be powerfully attractive.

Certainly, soup is the most versatile and variable item on the menu. It can be hot, chilled or jellied, delicate or hearty, clear or crammed with succulent morsels; and it may be served at any meal—as prelude, main dish, or even dessert—at any season of the year. Soups are also universally popular and reflect the rich diversity of tastes among the different nations of the world. We get borscht, hot or cold, from Russia, onion soup from France, a lemon-tanged soup from the Middle East, *soupe au pistou* —a savory vegetable melange scented with fresh basil and olive oil— from Mediterranean countries, and a salad soup, *gazpacho*, from Spain. From America come such creations as Georgia peanut soup, black bean soup and all kinds of zesty seafood chowders.

Generations weaned on the canned and dehydrated product, may find the notion of making soup from scratch novel—and perhaps forbidding. But, in fact, nothing could be simpler or more satisfying. Consider that virtually everything edible—meats, poultry, fish, all fruits and vegetables, the range of herbs, spices and seasonings—may be used in soup to good advantage, as a complement to any meal.

Among their other virtues, many soups can also be made quickly and well in advance of an important occasion. And hearty soups, like split pea and *gulyas* soup, are even better the second time around, so it pays to make them in quantity for more than one meal.

Soup Stock. Stock is sometimes called the soul or foundation of soup. Vegetable or fish stocks can be made in half an hour, and they are fine for certain purposes in soups that do not require long cooking. But the most flavorful stock for most uses is a meat stock, made by the long, slow simmering of meat; vegetables; chicken, veal or beef bones; and seasonings in water. An almost endless variety of soups can be prepared in a fairly short time just by adding a few additional ingredients to a lusty stock.

While classic French cuisine makes use of a dark brown beef stock (based on browned beef and beef bones), a light beef stock (based on veal bones and veal) and an even lighter one based on chicken, the last is actually sufficient for most soup-making requirements.

An excellent chicken stock can be made using the gizzard, carcass and natural pan juices of a roast chicken as a base, and filling out with vegetables, trimmings, parings and suitable leftovers and seasonings. In

1

fact, it is rich and hearty enough to substitute for beef stock in many recipes.

Making Stock. The preparation of a stock is simple, but certain procedures should be followed for best results. First, remove any fat from the meat and, to extract the most flavor from the ingredients, make sure they are all cool when the cooking begins. Start by combining the meat, bones and cold water in a stockpot and slowly bring the liquid to a simmer. For clear stock, do not mix cooked bones with uncooked bones, do not let the water boil, and skim off any foam that rises to the surface of the stock during the first 30 minutes of cooking. Then add the vegetables—usually carrots, leeks, celery and an onion pierced with a clove or two—and the seasonings. Starchy vegetables are avoided in stocks because they cause cloudiness and more rapid souring. Salt should be added in limited quantity because stock evaporates as it cooks, making the seasonings more concentrated. Salty flavor is also intensified if there is any wine in the stock. Partially cover the pot, to contain the heat and to keep it low enough to prevent boiling, and let the stock continue simmering about 7 to 8 hours for beef or veal, or 2 to 3 hours for chicken. Taste to see that the flavor is fully developed before removing the stock from the stove; reducing will concentrate the flavor.

When the stock is ready, pour it through a strainer, lined with a double layer of dampened cheesecloth, into a large bowl. Let it cool to room temperature, *uncovered*, and then refrigerate. The fat will rise to the surface and provide a protective coating on the top until the stock is used. Chilling is the most effective way of defatting stock, but, if time is at a premium, a shortcut can be taken: Wrap an ice cube in cheesecloth and skim it over the surface. The fat will congeal on contact with the ice and can then be easily lifted off.

Storing Stock. Stock is perishable and should be used within three or four days. If not used, bring it to a boil, allow it to cool (uncovered, as before) and refrigerate again. It should also be reheated if any additions are made to it during that time. Some people like to enrich the flavor and nutrition of stock by cooking an accumulation of vegetables, such as washed celery leaves, pea pods and parsley stems in water for 30 minutes, and adding this "pot likker" to it.

To freeze stock, pour it into containers of a size that will permit the greatest flexibility—anything from a cup to a quart. It's also extremely handy to freeze stock in ice cube trays and then transfer the cubes to a tightly closed plastic bag for storage in the freezer. Each small cube yields about 2 tablespoons of stock, a useful amount when only a small quantity is required for cooking vegetables or to perk up sauces.

Ready-to-Use Stocks and Concentrates. A number of canned, clear chicken or beef broths or bouillons can be substituted for homemade stock. They tend to be rather salty and some are overseasoned, so try several brands to determine your preference. Canned consommé tends to be rather sweet and strongly flavored and is not recommended for most re-

Food processor. The most efficient means of mincing, slicing, shredding and chopping large quantities of herbs and vegetables, or grating cheese for soups is a food processor with interchangeable disks and blades. Like a blender, it will also make a fine purée.

cipes. In a pinch, a good quality bouillon cube or bouillon powder will do, but watch the salt there, too.

The best solution, although somewhat more time consuming, is to simmer canned broth with an assortment of aromatic vegetables, seasonings, and, if possible, some chicken or beef bones. If you have a taste for chicken giblets, they may replace the bones; the liver is optional, again according to preference. To 5 or 6 cups of canned bouillon, add 2 leeks (including some of the green part) or 1 medium onion, 2 scraped carrots, a large celery stalk with its leaves, and a sprig or two of parsley. If available, add a few chicken parts or the giblets of 1 or 2 chickens (except the liver) to chicken bouillon or about 2 pounds of beef bones to beef bouillon. Simmer for 30 to 45 minutes, then skim and strain. The yield should be about a quart of full-flavored broth.

A Vocabulary of Soups. The names of soups are actually clues to how they are made. Strained and defatted clear stock, served as a soup, is usually called "broth" or, if it is beef, "bouillon" (from the French *bouillir*, meaning "to boil"). Consommé (also from a French word, which means "consummate") is chicken or beef stock that is additionally seasoned with

Electric blender. For fine purées, the basis of many cream soups, a blender works very well. Two speeds are sufficient; a jar with straight sides allows optimum circulation through the blades.

fragrant herbs, vegetables, and often meat, and further cooked down to concentrate its flavor. It is then clarified to sparkling brilliance by stirring in lightly beaten egg whites together with their finely crushed shells. As the stock simmers, the egg white solidifies and rises to the top of the pot carrying with it any small particles still floating in the stock. After careful straining, the result is indeed consummate, a limpid consommé.

Among the thick or opaque soups are purées, usually of vegetable or fruit, made with stock, water or wine and, if hot, enriched with butter. Potages are heavy soups based on vegetables that have been sautéed and then cooked in liquid before they are puréed. Cream soups are purées with cream added, and the term bisque generally refers to a cream soup made with shellfish. A velouté is based on a velouté sauce (a white sauce made with stock) and thickened with heavy cream and egg yolks. This type of soup must never be boiled or the eggs will curdle, and it should be reheated in a double boiler. Chowders are thick fish, meat or vegetable soups most typically made with milk and potatoes.

Many thick and some clear soups can be eaten cold and are even preferred that way. Those that are already thick will become even thicker when chilled, and can be thinned by adding more cream. Chilling can be sped up by putting the soup in the freezer.

Staless-steel chinois and tinned-steel food mill. For coarser purées than you can get in a blender, press food through the holes of a chinois, or choose one of three textures and crank the food through a mill like this one that attaches conveniently to any size bowl or pan.

Thickeners. For other variations, textures and flavors, soups may be thickened with a number of different ingredients. Rice or barley can be added to soup in the proportion of 1 teaspoon to a cup of liquid. To thicken a soup with flour, for each cup of liquid, mix 1½ teaspoons of flour with water to form a paste. Add these thickeners while the soup is simmering and enough in advance to cook them thoroughly before serving. Flour should cook 10 to 15 minutes to lose its "floury" taste.

Equipment. To make stock or large quantities of soup, nothing eases the task more than an ample stockpot. The ideal stockpot is tall and narrow, with a cover. The limited surface reduces the area from which evaporation can take place, and the height of the pot forces the liquid to boil up through the solid ingredients, allowing for greater flavor enrichment. Sturdy handles on either side help to keep the weight of the pot and its contents balanced when being lifted. While commercial stockpots can be found in sizes up to 100 quarts or more, most home kitchens can manage nicely with an 8- to 10-quart model, which will also serve for cooking such things as pasta, corn and lobsters. A stockpot should be made of a metal that is heavy enough to prevent scorching the food and that will not buckle with heat, but not so weighty as to be excessively difficult to move or lift when filled.

Stainless-steel stockpot. A large, deep stockpot with a heavy bottom and strong handles is ideal for the long, slow simmering of bones, meat and vegetables to make broth. Stainless steel won't affect the flavor of or discolor its contents, and it's easy to clean; aluminum sandwiched in the bottom prevents scorching.

Stainless-steel utensils. Large, strong tools with long handles are constantly needed for ladling, stirring and lifting solids from soups and broths. This ladle and skimmer hook onto the edge of the pot; the spoons have holes for hanging conveniently near the stove.

Heavy-duty aluminum would be an excellent choice for a stockpot, since its weight is reasonably light in relation to the thickness of the metal, and it's a good heat conductor. But aluminum interacts with acidic foods, causing them to darken and take on a metallic taste. Although somewhat heavier and more cumbersome than aluminum, a stainless-steel stockpot with an aluminum-clad or sandwich bottom offers equally good heat conduction and will not interfere with food.

Stockpots are, of course, admirable for making soup, particularly in large amounts. However, standard pots can certainly be used for soup making, provided they're reasonably heavy, large enough and have lids.

If a recipe doesn't specify an exact pot size, follow this rule of thumb: When soup ingredients are pureed or in small pieces, allow about 1 pint of pot capacity for each serving, or a 3-quart pot for 6 servings; when ingredients are bulky (e.g., large pieces of vegetable, meat, fish, etc.) allow up to 1 quart of pot capacity for each serving. In other words, for 6 servings, you'd need a 4- to 6-quart pot.

Other than a proper pot, soup making demands little special equipment. A sturdy cutting board, a paring knife, a chef's knife and a vegetable peeler will handle most peeling, cutting, chopping and slicing needs. Knives with blades made of no-stain, high-carbon steel are easy to maintain and can be kept very sharp.

A blender or a food processor (which also chops and slices) is useful for puréeing. However, if you like a little texture in puréed soup, and don't mind the slight time and effort involved, a hand-operated food mill does the job admirably and is preferred by many cooks.

A good-sized, sturdy strainer or chinois is indispensable for separating liquids from solids, and is also used for puréeing. Incidentally, if you find it awkward to pour from a large stock or soup pot into a strainer, use a small saucepan (1 or 1½ quarts) as a ladle to transfer the soup.

You will also need a large, shallow, long-handled spoon for skimming, a slotted spoon for lifting smaller bits from the pot in the course of cooking, and, of course, an ample ladle if you want to serve from the pot.

Serving. Soup seems even more inviting when ladled out at the table from an ample tureen or casserole. In fact, many cooks like to prepare slow-simmering soups in ceramic pots, since they can go from range to table—doubling as serving pieces. Do exercise caution, however, when using such pots over direct heat—even if they're labeled "flameproof." Keep the heat low, and slip an asbestos mat under the pot—which should be at least one-third full before it is set over the heat. It's better to be safe then sorry.

Hot soups will stay hot longer if both tureen and bowl are prewarmed before filling, and if the tureen has a lid. Similarly, cold soups hold their icy snap to the last spoonful if the bowls are chilled in advance.

Seafood Soups

CUBAN FISH CHOWDER

Eliza and Joshua Baer

2 servings

This is a hot chowder. We learned about it from an exiled Cuban gentleman named Angelo Perez who still makes the chowder at his rooming house in Arecibo, Puerto Rico. To serve more people, double the proportions for five and triple them for eight.

2 RED ONIONS, FINELY CHOPPED
3 TABLESPOONS OLIVE OIL
1 TABLESPOON ANNATTO OIL (AVAIL-ABLE IN HISPANIC MARKETS)
2 CLOVES GARLIC, FINELY CHOPPED
2 RED BELL PEPPERS, COARSELY CHOPPED
1 TEASPOON GROUND CUMIN
SALT
¼ TEASPOON CAYENNE PEPPER
½ TEASPOON THYME
½ TEASPOON OREGANO
1 POUND FILLETS OF RED SNAPPER, LING COD OR ANY OTHER FIRM WHITE FISH (EXCEPT SOLE)

2 TABLESPOONS LIME JUICE, AP-PROXIMATELY
2 RIPE TOMATOES, PEELED, SEEDED AND COARSELY CHOPPED
1 OR 2 TABLESPOONS DARK RUM
1 CUP DRY SHERRY OR DRY WHITE WINE, APPROXIMATELY
¼ CUP CHOPPED PARSLEY
LIME SLICES
AVOCADO SLICES

1. In a heavy enameled casserole, sauté the chopped onions in the olive and annatto oils until the onions are golden and soft.

2. Add the garlic, red peppers, cumin, 1 teaspoon of salt, cayenne, thyme and oregano. Sauté the mixture until the peppers begin to soften.

   Note: Be sure to add the salt and cayenne at the same time; the cayenne will not taste as "hot" without salt.

3. Add the fish fillets, 2 tablespoons of lime juice, tomatoes, rum and 1 cup of sherry (or white wine). Bring the chowder to a slow boil, stirring constantly and making sure that nothing sticks to the bottom of the casserole. As the fish fillets cook, break them into smaller and smaller chunks with a wooden spoon.

4. Cover the casserole and allow it to simmer very slowly for at least 30 minutes. Taste and add more salt, lime juice or sherry if the chowder tastes too flat. Turn off the heat and stir in the chopped parsley.

5. Allow the chowder to sit, covered, for another 30 minutes. Then reheat it slowly until it barely reaches a boil.

   Note: Turning the heat under the chowder on and off makes a better blend of the flavors.

6. Turn off the heat, let it sit for 5 minutes, and then serve in large bowls accompanied by slices of lime and avocado, on a separate plate, and hot French bread.

Note: You can add milk or cream to this recipe 10 minutes before serving, but then it becomes more like a New England chowder than a Cuban chowder.

CALIFORNIA CIOPPINO

Emanuel and Madeline Greenberg

6 to 8 servings

Here is America's answer to France's *bouillabaisse* and Italy's *zuppa di pesce*.

4 TO 6 TABLESPOONS OLIVE OIL
1 LARGE ONION, CHOPPED
1 MEDIUM-SIZED GREEN PEPPER, CHOPPED
3 TO 4 CLOVES GARLIC, MINCED
1 LARGE CAN (2 POUNDS, 3 OUNCES) ITALIAN PLUM TOMATOES WITH BASIL
1 CAN (6 OUNCES) TOMATO PASTE
2 CUPS DRY RED WINE
½ CUP CHOPPED FRESH PARSLEY
1 TEASPOON DRIED BASIL
1 TEASPOON OREGANO
SALT, TO TASTE
PEPPER, TO TASTE
2 POUNDS MIXED, FIRM, WHITE FISH FILLETS (SEA BASS, HALIBUT, ROCKFISH, COD, ETC.) CUT UP
1 POUND RAW SHRIMP, SHELLED AND DEVEINED
2 TO 3 POUNDS FRESH DUNGENESS OR BLUE CRABS IN SHELL, CUT INTO LARGE PIECES*
8 TABLESPOONS (1 STICK) BUTTER
2 CLOVES GARLIC, CRUSHED
1 LOAF FRENCH OR ITALIAN BREAD
1 DOZEN CLAMS, WELL RINSED
2 DOZEN MUSSELS, WELL CRUSHED

1. In a large, flameproof casserole (preferably one that can go to the table), heat 4 tablespoons of olive oil. Add the onion, green pepper and garlic. Cook, stirring occasionally, until the vegetables have softened. Add a little more oil if necessary.

2. Preheat the oven to 400 F.

3. Add the tomatoes, tomato paste, wine, herbs, salt and pepper. Bring the mixture to a boil, then cover, reduce the heat and simmer about 20 minutes.

4. Add the fish, shrimp and crabs. Simmer for 20 to 25 minutes, until the fish is just cooked.

5. Meanwhile, make the garlic bread. Cream the butter with the crushed garlic cloves.

6. Make crosswise cuts in the loaf of bread at 1'' intervals, a little more than half-way through it. Spread the garlic-butter mixture on either side of each slice of bread. Bake in the preheated oven for 10 minutes, or until golden brown.

Continued from preceding page

7. Meanwhile, add the clams and mussels to the soup. Simmer until they open, 5 to 10 minutes longer.

8. Bring the casserole of *cioppino* to the table with a basket of the garlic bread. Put a slice of garlic bread in each soup plate and ladle the soup over it.

* The crab should be cut up as close to cooking time as possible.

THE "21" CLUB MANHATTAN CLAM CHOWDER

Emanuel and Madeline Greenberg

6 servings

The recipe below is a house specialty of New York's The "21" Club and it's about as good as this soup can be.

18 LARGE, HARD-SHELL CHOWDER
  CLAMS, WELL RINSED
2 SMALL STALKS CELERY
1½ TEASPOONS PEPPERCORNS
6 CUPS WATER
¼ CUP CLARIFIED BUTTER*
1 CUP DICED, PEELED POTATOES
½ CUP DICED CELERY
½ CUP DICED ONION
¼ CUP DICED LEEKS (INCLUDING
  SOME OF THE GREEN PART)

¼ CUP FLOUR
2 TABLESPOONS TOMATO PASTE
1 CUP WELL DRAINED, CANNED TO-
  MATOES, CHOPPED
½ CUP CHICKEN STOCK
1 TABLESPOON DRIED THYME
SALT, TO TASTE
PEPPER, TO TASTE

1. In a large pot with a lid, place the clams, celery stalks, peppercorns and water. Cover, bring to a boil, and simmer until the clams open.

2. Pour the liquid through a strainer lined with a dampened linen cloth that has been rinsed and wrung out. Reserve the liquid.

3. Chop the clams and set them aside.

4. In the same pot, heat the clarified butter. Add the diced potatoes, celery, onion and leek and sauté them until glazed. Stir in the flour. Cook, stirring, until the flour is thoroughly mixed with the vegetables.

5. Add the reserved clam broth, tomato paste and tomatoes. Mix well. Simmer about 1½ hours.

6. In a small saucepan, combine the chicken stock and thyme. Bring to a simmer over low heat, cover and cook for 10 minutes. Strain the mixture into the soup.

   Note: The thyme is simmered in the stock just briefly to prevent it from dominating the chowder.

7. Add the chopped clams. Simmer for 30 minutes, then season with salt and pepper.

8. Serve the chowder with Pilot crackers or any other large, plain, white cracker.

Note: If you'd like the chowder a little thicker, stir 1 or 2 tablespoons of flour into ¼ cup of cold water and add this mixture at the same time as the strained chicken stock.

* To clarify the butter, melt about 6 tablespoons of butter in a small saucepan set over low heat. Remove the butter from the heat and skim the foam from the top. Let the butter stand a few minutes, then pour off the clear golden liquid, leaving the milky sediment at the bottom of the pan.

PROVENÇAL FISH SOUP

Nan Mabon

6 to 8 servings

½ TEASPOON FENNEL SEEDS
1 IMPORTED BAY LEAF
2 SPRIGS FRESH PARSLEY
4 FRESH BASIL LEAVES OR ½ TEA-
   SPOON DRIED BASIL
5 MEDIUM-SIZED LEEKS
2 TABLESPOONS OLIVE OIL
3 LARGE CLOVES GARLIC, PEELED
   AND FINELY MINCED
1 CAN (2 POUNDS) IMPORTED ITALIAN
   TOMATOES

6 CUPS FISH OR CHICKEN STOCK
LARGE PINCH OF SAFFRON POWDER
1½ POUNDS RED SNAPPER AND COD
   FILLETS, CUT INTO SMALL SQUARES
SALT
FRESHLY GROUND BLACK PEPPER
2 TABLESPOONS FINELY CHOPPED
   PARSLEY

1. Place the fennel, bay leaf, parsley sprigs and basil in the center of a small square of cheesecloth and tie them into a packet with string.

2. Cut the leeks into ¼"-thick slices and cover them with cold water. Separate the concentric circles of the leek slices to make certain all the sand is removed. Drain well.

3. In a deep casserole, heat the olive oil. Add the leeks and toss them in the oil to coat, cover and cook over low heat for about 5 minutes.

4. Stir in the garlic, cook for a minute and then add the tomatoes and their juice. Bring to a boil.

5. Add the stock, herb packet and the saffron. Cook, partially covered, over low heat for 25 minutes. (The soup can be prepared ahead of time to this point.)

6. About 10 minutes before serving, reheat the soup and add the fish and salt and pepper to taste. Cook for 5 minutes over medium heat; then stir, breaking up the fish into smaller pieces.

7. Serve the soup immediately, garnished with the chopped parsley. Have plenty of French bread and sweet butter on the table.

Note: If you reheat this soup the next day, take care not to let it cook too long because the fish will toughen.

FIRE ISLAND SCALLOP CHOWDER

Emanuel and Madeline Greenberg

4 to 6 servings

1 POUND BAY SCALLOPS*
3 CUPS HALF-AND-HALF OR MILK
1 CUP CLAM JUICE
3 TABLESPOONS BUTTER
1 SMALL ONION, CHOPPED (APPROX-
   IMATELY ¼ CUP)
1 SMALL CLOVE GARLIC, MINCED

1 TABLESPOON FLOUR
2 MEDIUM-SIZED POTATOES, PEELED
   AND DICED (APPROXIMATELY 1½
   CUPS)
PINCH OF NUTMEG
SALT, TO TASTE
PEPPER, TO TASTE

1. Rinse the scallops quickly and pat them dry with paper towels.

2. In a saucepan, combine the half-and-half (or milk) and clam juice and bring to a simmer over low heat.

3. In a larger saucepan, melt the butter. Add the onion and garlic and sauté over low heat until they have softened.

4. Stir in the flour and continue to cook for 2 to 3 minutes.

5. Slowly stir in the warmed liquids. Bring the mixture just to the boiling point; then add the potatoes and simmer for 10 minutes.

6. Add the scallops, nutmeg, salt and pepper. Cook until the potatoes and scallops are tender, about 6 to 8 minutes. Taste and correct the seasoning, if necessary.

* Sea scallops may be used, but they won't be as tender. After rinsing and drying, cut them into pieces the size of bay scallops.

CREAM OF MUSSEL SOUP (BILLI-BI)

Ruth Spear

8 servings

Originally served at Maxim's in Paris, this soup was a favorite of William B. Leeds, a wealthy American tin magnate and *habitué* of the restaurant. Craig Claiborne calls it "perhaps the greatest soup ever created."

1 CUP CHOPPED ONIONS
¼ CUP CHOPPED SHALLOTS
4 TABLESPOONS (½ STICK) BUTTER
1½ CUPS DRY WHITE WINE
4 SPRIGS PARSLEY
4 POUNDS MUSSELS, CLEANED AND
   DEBEARDED

1 CUP MILK
2 EGG YOLKS
2 CUPS HEAVY CREAM
½ TEASPOON SALT
FRESHLY GROUND BLACK PEPPER,
   TO TASTE
1 TABLESPOON CHOPPED PARSLEY

1. In a heavy soup pot, combine the onions, shallots, butter, wine and parsley

sprigs. Lay the mussels on this bed, cover tightly, bring the liquid to a boil and steam for 8 to 10 minutes over high heat, or until the mussels have opened.

2. With a slotted spoon, scoop the mussels out of the pot and set aside.

3. Carefully strain the broth through a piece of cheesecloth into a bowl. Press down on the vegetables to extract all their juices.

4. Shell the mussels, discarding any that are unopened, and cut or pull away the black tissue around the outside edges.

5. Reserve 24 of the yellow centers of the mussels and purée the rest, along with the strained broth, in a blender or food processor.

6. Pour the purée into the top part of a double boiler and set it over hot water.

7. Add the milk and heat to scalding.

8. In a small bowl, beat the egg yolks with the cream; then, stirring constantly, add a few tablespoons of the hot mussel mixture. Stir the egg yolk mixture into the soup, and continue stirring constantly, until the soup has thickened slightly. Season with salt and pepper.

9. Remove the soup from the heat and serve in individual bowls, adding 3 of the reserved mussels to each portion and garnishing it with minced parsley.

Note: To serve the soup cold, place the pan over cold water to cool it quickly. Then refrigerate. Thin with a little light cream before serving, if necessary. Garnish as for the hot soup.

NEW ENGLAND CLAM CHOWDER

Emanuel and Madeline Greenberg

6 to 8 servings

Authentic recipes for New England clam chowder have one thing in common—they are *not* thickened with flour.

2 DOZEN LARGE HARD-SHELL CLAMS,
   WELL RINSED
2 CUPS WATER
¼ POUND SALT PORK, DICED
1 MEDIUM-SIZED ONION, CHOPPED
4 MEDIUM-SIZED POTATOES, PEELED
   AND DICED
PINCH OF DRIED THYME
SALT, TO TASTE
PEPPER, TO TASTE
4 CUPS HALF-AND-HALF
2 TABLESPOONS BUTTER

1. In a heavy, 2½-quart pot, combine the clams and 2 cups of water. Cover the pot and bring the water to a boil; reduce the heat and simmer until the clams open.

2. Strain the liquid into a bowl and reserve it.

Continued from preceding page

3. Remove the clams from their shells, chop them and set aside.

4. In the same pot, heat the salt pork until the fat is rendered and the scraps are brown and crisp. Lift out the scraps (cracklings) and set them aside.

5. Add the onion to the pot and cook until softened.

6. Measure the clam broth and, if necessary, add enough water to it to make 3½ cups. Add the broth, potatoes, thyme, salt and pepper to the pot.

7. Bring the mixture to a boil. Partially cover the pot and reduce the heat; simmer until the potatoes are tender, about 15 minutes.

8. Add the half-and-half, chopped clams and butter to the pan. Bring the chowder just to a boil. Taste for seasoning.

9. To serve, garnish each portion of chowder with some salt pork cracklings and accompany with Common* (as they are known in New England) crackers.

* A large, rather dense, unsalted white cracker.

CLAM BISQUE

Florence Fabricant

4 servings

1 DOZEN CHERRYSTONE CLAMS WITH
   THEIR JUICES
2 TABLESPOONS BUTTER
½ CUP FINELY MINCED ONION
2 TABLESPOONS FLOUR
1 CUP MILK, SCALDED
2 TEASPOONS TOMATO PASTE
½ CUP HEAVY CREAM
SALT, TO TASTE
CAYENNE PEPPER
2 TEASPOONS FINELY MINCED CHIVES

1. Open the clams (or have them opened) and drain them thoroughly, reserving *all* the juice. If you don't have 1½ to 2 cups of fresh clam juice, supplement it with bottled clam juice.

2. Purée the clams in a blender or food processor. To do this in a blender, you may have to chop the clams first.

3. Refrigerate the clams and clam juice until ready to use.

4. In a heavy saucepan, melt the butter, add the onion and sauté it just until soft.

5. Stir in the flour and cook for 2 to 3 minutes.

6. Stir in the milk and continue stirring with a whisk until the mixture thickens, about 5 minutes.

7. Stir in the clam juice; then add the clam purée. Stir until smooth and reduce the heat to a simmer.

8. Dissolve the tomato paste in the cream and stir into the clam mixture. Taste for salt.

9. Remove the soup from the heat and serve, dusted with a little cayenne and some chives. Because the soup is rich, it is best served as a first course preceding a light entrée such as grilled chicken or a veal sauté. A muscadet wine suits it best.

GLOUCESTER GOLD

Emanuel and Madeline Greenberg

4 to 6 servings

½ CUP OLIVE OIL
2 MEDIUM-SIZED ONIONS, CHOPPED
3 CELERY STALKS, CHOPPED
1 LARGE CARROT, SCRAPED AND
  THINLY SLICED
2 CLOVES GARLIC, CRUSHED
2 CUPS CLAM JUICE
2 CUPS TOMATO JUICE
1 CUP DRY WHITE WINE
½ CUP PEAS, FRESH OR FROZEN
¼ CUP COARSELY CHOPPED PARSLEY
1 POUND BONELESS HALIBUT OR
  OTHER FIRM WHITE FISH, CUT INTO
  BITE-SIZED CUBES

FOUR TO SIX ½"-THICK SLICES
  CRUSTY FRENCH OR ITALIAN
  BREAD
1 OR 2 CLOVES GARLIC, CUT IN HALF
¼ TO ⅓ CUP GRATED PARMESAN OR
  SWISS CHEESE
¾ POUND RAW SHRIMP, SHELLED
  AND DEVEINED
½ TEASPOON THYME
¼ TEASPOON BASIL
SALT, TO TASTE
PEPPER, TO TASTE

1. In a large pot, heat ¼ cup of the oil. Add the onions, celery and carrot and sauté until the onions have softened, but are not browned.

2. Preheat the oven to 350 F.

3. Add the crushed garlic, clam juice, tomato juice, wine, peas and parsley to the sautéing vegetables. Bring the mixture to a simmer and add the halibut. Simmer about 10 minutes longer.

4. Meanwhile, prepare the croutons, one slice for each serving. Rub the crust of each slice of bread with the cut garlic, then brush both sides of the slice with the remaining olive oil. Bake until golden in the preheated oven, about 8 to 10 minutes. Remove the bread from the oven, turn the slices over and sprinkle them with the cheese. Set them aside, but leave the oven at 350 F.

5. Add the shrimp, thyme, basil, salt and pepper to the soup pot. Simmer for 5 to 7 minutes longer, or just until the shrimp turn pink.

6. About 4 minutes before the shrimp are done, return the croutons to the oven and bake until the cheese melts.

7. To serve, put a hot garlic crouton in each soup bowl and ladle the soup over it.

Meat and Poultry Soups

HEARTY VEGETABLE-BEEF SOUP

Emanuel and Madeline Greenberg

8 servings

This is a two-stage recipe: First, the beef stock is prepared, then the vegetables are cooked in the stock to make the soup.

Beef Stock:
2 POUNDS BEEF SHIN AND MARROW BONES, CRACKED
1 LARGE ONION, QUARTERED
3 QUARTS WATER
1½ TO 2 POUNDS BONELESS BEEF (IN ONE PIECE)
2 CARROTS, SCRAPED
1 STALK CELERY WITH LEAVES, CHOPPED
2 TO 3 SPRIGS PARSLEY
1 BAY LEAF
1 TABLESPOON SALT
6 PEPPERCORNS

Other Soup Ingredients:
1 MEDIUM-SIZED ONION, SLICED

3 CARROTS, SCRAPED AND DICED
1 CUP PEELED AND DICED POTATOES
1 CUP CUT GREEN BEANS
1 CUP CORN KERNELS (FRESH OR CANNED)
1 CUP GREEN PEAS (FRESH OR FROZEN)
1 CUP CELERY, SLICED
1 CAN (16 OUNCES) TOMATOES, UN-DRAINED AND BROKEN UP
1 CLOVE GARLIC, CRUSHED
2 TO 3 SPRIGS PARSLEY, MINCED
1 TEASPOON DRIED BASIL
SALT, TO TASTE
PEPPER, TO TASTE

1. Preheat the oven to 425 F.

2. Place the bones and onion in a shallow baking pan and bake for 45 minutes. Transfer the bones and onion to a large stockpot.

3. Pour 2 cups of the water into the baking pan, set it over low heat and stir to loosen any brown bits that cling to the bottom of the pan. Pour the water from the pan into the stockpot. Add the rest of the water and the remaining ingredients for the stock. Bring to a boil; skim off the scum rising to the surface. Partially cover the pot, reduce the heat and simmer for 2 hours.

4. Remove the beef from the pot and set it aside. Strain the stock and skim off the fat. (Or strain, cool and refrigerate the stock, and then lift off the hardened fat.)

5. Trim and cube the beef and reserve it.

6. Pour the beef stock into a large pot. Add the reserved beef and other soup in-

gredients and bring the mixture to a boil. Cover and reduce the heat; simmer for 1 hour, or until all of the vegetables are tender.

7. Taste, correct the seasoning, if necessary, and serve.

Note: Although it won't be the same, you can shorten the cooking time considerably by using canned beef stock and adding any cooked, cubed meat or poultry you have on hand. Also, other vegetables, such as turnips, shredded cabbage, zucchini and lima beans, can be added or substituted for the ones listed in the recipe.

CHICKEN STOCK

Emanuel and Madeline Greenberg

2½ to 3 quarts

The most versatile stock for soups is one made of chicken, and it is perfectly permissible to use leftover chicken bones or carcasses

2 ROAST CHICKEN CARCASSES (SKIN, BONES, BITS OF MEAT)
GIBLETS (EXCEPT LIVERS) OF 2 CHICKENS
PAN JUICES (ONLY THE SKIMMED, NATURAL PAN JUICES—NOT GRAVY OR SAUCE)
1 MEDIUM-SIZED ONION

1 CARROT, SCRAPED
1 STALK CELERY (WITH LEAVES)
1 LEEK (WITH SOME OF THE GREEN)
1 PARSNIP
3 SPRIGS PARSLEY
1 PARSLEY ROOT, IF AVAILABLE
SPRIG OF DILL
2 TEASPOONS SALT

1. Put all the ingredients in a 5- to 6-quart pot. Add water to within ½" of the top of the pot. Cover, leaving the lid slightly askew, and bring to a boil; reduce the heat and simmer about 2 hours, skimming occasionally.

2. Pour the liquid through a fine strainer and let it cool to room temperature.

   Note: For extra clear stock, line the strainer with cheesecloth that has first been rinsed in cold water.

3. Refrigerate the cooled stock.

4. Before using, remove any congealed fat on the top.

Note: This recipe is merely a guide. Feel free to add or change ingredients, accommodating your own taste, and whatever comes to hand. If you have only one chicken carcass, for instance, you can supplement with a couple of pounds of uncooked chicken backs and necks. A roast turkey frame can stand in for the chicken, and vegetables may be varied, depending on what's available. Incidentally, you don't have to make stock the day after you've served roast chicken. Pop the leftovers into the freezer, along with the giblets, and do the stock whenever you find it's convenient.

LEMON SOUP (AVGOLEMONO)

Carol Cutler

8 servings

6 CUPS WELL-SEASONED CHICKEN
   STOCK
1 CUP COOKED RICE, OR ⅓ CUP RAW
   RICE
3 EGGS, ROOM TEMPERATURE
¼ TO ½ CUP LEMON JUICE, ROOM
   TEMPERATURE
SALT, TO TASTE
PEPPER, TO TASTE
DASH OF TABASCO SAUCE

1. In a large pot, heat the stock, then add the cooked rice and bring to a slow simmer. If raw rice is used, cover and simmer for 20 minutes.

2. Break the eggs in a bowl and beat with a whisk. Pour in ¼ cup of the lemon juice, add salt, pepper and Tabasco and beat again.

   Note: By having the eggs and lemon juice at room temperature and beating them together, you reduce the risk of curdling the eggs.

3. Pour the egg-lemon mixture very slowly into the simmering soup while whisking constantly and rapidly. Keep the liquid just under the boiling point. Taste for lemon flavor and adjust accordingly. Likewise, correct the amounts of salt and pepper, if necessary.

4. Serve the soup while it is very hot in individual soup cups, making certain that each portion contains some rice.

HUNGARIAN GOULASH SOUP (GULYÁS MAGYAR)

Maria Luisa Scott and Jack Denton Scott

6 to 8 servings

2 TABLESPOONS BUTTER
1½ POUNDS LEAN BEEF CHUCK, CUT
   INTO 1" CUBES
1 LARGE YELLOW ONION, THINLY
   SLICED
1 TEASPOON SALT
2 TABLESPOONS CRUSHED CARAWAY
   SEEDS
2 MEDIUM-SIZED RIPE TOMATOES,
   PEELED, SEEDED AND DICED, OR
   1½ CUPS CANNED TOMATOES,
   DRAINED AND COARSELY CHOPPED

2 SWEET RED PEPPERS, SEEDED, DE-
   RIBBED AND DICED
7 CUPS BEEF BROTH
2 MEDIUM-SIZED POTATOES, DICED
½ TEASPOON DRIED THYME
1 TEASPOON BLACK PEPPER
1½ TEASPOONS HUNGARIAN PAPRIKA

1. In a large pot, melt the butter. Add the beef and brown it.

2. Add the onion and cook for 5 minutes.

3. Stir in the salt and caraway seeds. Cover and simmer for 25 minutes.

4. Stir in the tomatoes and peppers and ½ cup of the beef broth. Cover and simmer, stirring occasionally, for 40 minutes. Add a little more broth from time to time, as needed.

5. Add the potatoes, remaining beef broth, thyme, black pepper and paprika and stir well. Cover and simmer for 30 minutes, or until the meat and potatoes are fork tender.

6. Taste for seasoning and serve.

Note: If you like, do as the Hungarians and Austrians do and add ¼ pound cooked and drained thin noodles to the soup just before serving and accompany the soup with plenty of crusty bread and cold beer. The Austrians also favor a young red wine as the beverage.

PHILADELPHIA PEPPERPOT

Emanuel and Madeline Greenberg

8 servings

2 POUNDS VEAL KNUCKLE
¾ POUND FRESH TRIPE, DICED
1 TEASPOON PEPPERCORNS
¼ TEASPOON WHOLE CLOVES
3 QUARTS WATER
3 MEDIUM-SIZED ONIONS, DICED
1½ TEASPOONS SALT
3 TABLESPOONS BUTTER
2 GREEN PEPPERS, DICED

3 MEDIUM-SIZED BEETS, PEELED AND DICED
2 SPRIGS PARSLEY
½ TEASPOON BASIL
¼ TEASPOON THYME
¼ TEASPOON MARJORAM
⅓ CUP RICE
1 CAN (16 OUNCES) WHOLE TOMATOES

1. Place the veal knuckle and tripe in a large pot. Tie the peppercorns and cloves together in a piece of cheesecloth and add them to the pot, along with 3 quarts of water, and one of the onions. Bring to a boil. Add the salt, cover, reduce the heat and simmer for 2 hours.

2. In a skillet, heat the butter. Add the remaining onions, green peppers and beets. Sauté the vegetables for about 10 minutes, or until they are lightly browned.

3. Add the vegetables to the soup along with the parsley, herbs and rice. Cover and cook for 30 minutes.

4. Break up the tomatoes and add them, together with their juices, to the soup pot. Cook for 10 minutes more.

5. Remove the spice bag and the veal knuckle from the pot. Skim the fat from the soup and taste for seasoning.

6. Cut the meat from the bone, dice it and return it to the soup; reheat and serve.

MULLED CLARET CONSOMMÉ

Emanuel and Madeline Greenberg

6 servings

1½ CUPS GOOD, DRY RED WINE
  (SUCH AS ZINFANDEL OR BURGUNDY)
ONE 3"- TO 4"-LONG STICK CINNAMON
2 TEASPOONS SUGAR
4 CUPS CLEAR BEEF STOCK
6 THIN LEMON SLICES
6 CLOVES

1. In a glass or enameled saucepan, combine the wine, cinnamon stick and sugar. Bring the mixture just to a boil, then remove it from the heat. Cover and let it stand about 2 hours.

2. Pour the beef stock into a second saucepan. Strain the spiced wine into it and heat the mixture to the boiling point.

3. Serve, garnishing each portion with a lemon slice studded with a whole clove in the center.

HOT-SOUR SOUP

Gloria Bley Miller

4 servings

4 DRIED BLACK CHINESE MUSHROOMS
  (AVAILABLE IN ORIENTAL MARKETS)
2 OUNCES LEAN PORK
6 RAW SHRIMP
1 SCALLION
2 EGGS
1 TABLESPOON CORNSTARCH
3 TABLESPOONS WATER
1½ TABLESPOONS WHITE VINEGAR

1 TABLESPOON SOY SAUCE
¼ TEASPOON SALT
¼ TEASPOON WHITE PEPPER
6 CUPS CHICKEN STOCK
¼ CUP BAMBOO SHOOTS, CUT INTO
  ¼" x ⅛" STRIPS
6 SNOW PEAS, CUT INTO ⅛"-WIDE
  STRIPS
½ TEASPOON TABASCO SAUCE

1. Soften the dried black mushrooms in enough hot water to cover for 30 minutes.

2. Cut the pork across the grain into ¼"-thick slices, then cut the slices into ⅛" strips.

3. Shell and devein the shrimp.

4. Squeeze the excess liquid from the soaked mushrooms, remove their stems, and then cut the caps into strips.

5. Mince the scallion.

6. In a cup, beat the eggs lightly.

7. In another cup, combine the cornstarch and 3 tablespoons of water, blending well.

8. In a third cup, combine the vinegar, soy sauce, salt and pepper.

9. In a soup pot, bring the stock to a boil. Add the pork, bamboo shoots and mushroom strips. Bring to a boil again. Reduce the heat and simmer, covered, for 15 minutes. Skim the soup if necessary.

10. Add the shrimp to the stock.

11. Restir the vinegar-soy mixture and stir it into the soup until it is well blended.

12. Next, stir the cornstarch mixture again and add it to the soup, stirring constantly, until the soup thickens, about 2 minutes more.

13. Then, add the scallion, the snow pea strips, and the Tabasco sauce.

14. Finally, re-beat the egg and add it in a thin stream to the soup while stirring to form yellow threads as the egg sets. Serve at once.

Note: For contrast, this soup should be followed by bland food. For lunch, it might be served with a delicate omelet. For dinner, it might be followed by a lightly-seasoned roast or steamed chicken dish.

ZUPPA ROMANA

Emanuel and Madeline Greenberg

4 to 6 servings

2 TABLESPOONS OLIVE OIL
2 LARGE ONIONS, THINLY SLICED
1 CLOVE GARLIC, MINCED
¼ POUND PIECE *PROSCIUTTO*, CHOPPED
1 CAN (16 OUNCES) WHOLE TOMATOES, DRAINED AND BROKEN UP
½ CUP DRY WHITE WINE
6 CUPS BEEF OR CHICKEN STOCK
3 MEDIUM-SIZED POTATOES, PEELED AND QUARTERED

$\frac{1}{8}$ TEASPOON OREGANO
$\frac{1}{8}$ TEASPOON THYME
SALT, TO TASTE
PEPPER, TO TASTE
2 EGG YOLKS
¼ CUP CHOPPED PARSLEY
¼ CUP GRATED PARMESAN OR ROMANO CHEESE, PLUS ADDITIONAL CHEESE FOR THE TABLE

1. In a large pot, heat the olive oil. Add the onions and garlic and cook slowly until they are golden.

2. Add the *prosciutto* and tomatoes to the pot. Cook, stirring, for about 3 minutes.

3. Then add the white wine, stock, potatoes, herbs, salt and pepper. Bring the mixture to a boil; cover, reduce the heat and simmer until the potatoes are soft, about 20 to 25 minutes.

4. Beat the egg yolks together with the parsley and grated cheese. Beat in 2 or 3 tablespoons of hot soup, then stir the egg mixture into the soup.

5. Simmer a few minutes longer, stirring. Serve hot with additional cheese.

VERMONT CHEDDAR CHEESE SOUP

Emanuel and Madeline Greenberg

6 to 8 servings

3 TABLESPOONS BUTTER
3 SCALLIONS (INCLUDING SOME OF
   THE GREEN PART), CHOPPED
½ MEDIUM-SIZED ONION, CHOPPED
1 STALK CELERY, CHOPPED
3 TABLESPOONS FLOUR
1/8 TEASPOON NUTMEG

1/8 TEASPOON PEPPER
2 CUPS CHICKEN STOCK
4 CUPS MILK
6 OUNCES CHEDDAR CHEESE*,
   SHREDDED
SALT, TO TASTE
DASH OF WORCESTERSHIRE SAUCE

1. In a large pot, melt the butter. Add the scallions, onion and celery. Cook until the onion softens.

2. Stir in the flour, nutmeg and pepper and cook for 2 or 3 minutes longer.

3. Gradually stir in the stock. Bring it to a boil; cover, reduce the heat and simmer for 15 minutes. Cool the mixture slightly, then strain and return it to the pan.

4. Add the milk and bring it just to a boil.

5. Gradually add the cheese, stirring to melt it before adding more. Return the soup just to a boil, stirring often.

6. Taste for seasoning, and add salt and Worcestershire sauce.

* For a fuller cheese taste, used an aged "sharp" cheddar.

OXTAIL AND VEGETABLE SOUP

Elizabeth Schneider Colchie

6 servings

3 POUNDS OXTAIL, CUT UP AND
   TRIMMED OF FAT
2 MEDIUM-SIZED CARROTS, PEELED
   AND QUARTERED
1 TEASPOON MARJORAM
1 TABLESPOON SALT
2 TABLESPOONS LARD
2 TO 3 CUPS DICED RED AND GREEN
   BELL PEPPERS
4 CUPS SLICED ONIONS

4 CUPS (ABOUT 1 TO 1½ POUNDS)
   SLICED CABBAGE, APPROXIMATELY
1½ TABLESPOONS SWEET HUNGARI-
   AN PAPRIKA
1 TEASPOON MINCED GARLIC
¼ CUP FLOUR
PEPPER, TO TASTE
2 TO 3 TABLESPOONS FINELY MINCED
   DILL

1. In a large kettle, place the oxtail with enough water to cover it. Bring the water to a boil, reduce the heat and simmer for 2 to 3 minutes. Drain the meat and rinse both it and the pot. Return the meat to the pot.

2. Add the carrots, marjoram, salt and 3½ quarts of water to the pot and simmer

for 1 hour.

3. In a large skillet, melt the lard; add the peppers, onions and cabbage and cook over moderate heat until the vegetables have wilted.

4. Add the paprika, garlic and flour and stir for a few minutes.

5. Add a few cups of the broth to the skillet and stir over moderate heat until the mixture is smooth; then pour it in with the oxtail and broth and simmer, partly covered, for 2 hours, or until the meat is nearly falling from the bones. Season with pepper.

5. Skim off some, but not all of the fat. Add the minced dill.

6. Serve, if you like, with an accompaniment of sour cream, yogurt, dill and salt and pepper to taste mixed together in a separate bowl.

Note: As with most hearty peasant soups, this soup improves if refrigerated overnight and reheated the next day.

THE FOUR SEASONS LENTIL-SAUSAGE SOUP

Emanuel and Madeline Greenberg

8 servings

1 POUND LENTILS
1 LARGE POTATO, PEELED
1 MEDIUM-SIZED ONION, PEELED
1 BAY LEAF
1 TABLESPOON SALT, OR TO TASTE
2 QUARTS WATER
2 CUPS MILK
2 CUPS LIGHT CREAM
2 TABLESPOONS OIL
12 *CHIPOLATA* SAUSAGES*, SLICED

1. Soak the lentils in cold water overnight.

2. Drain the lentils and put them in a large pot. Add the potato, onion, bay leaf, salt and 2 quarts of water. Bring to a boil; cover, reduce the heat and simmer for 2 to 3 hours, or until the lentils are very tender.

3. Remove and discard the bay leaf. Purée the soup in a blender, 2 cups at a time, or push it through a sieve.

4. Return the purée to the pot. Stir in the milk and cream. Bring it to a simmer.

5. Meanwhile, heat the oil in a skillet, add the sliced sausages and sauté them, turning occasionally, until they are browned on both sides.

6. Add the sausage to the soup, simmer for 5 minutes longer and serve.

* If *chipolata* sausages are unavailable, ½ pound of sweet Italian sausages may be substituted.

CHICKEN EGG-DROP SOUP (STRACIATELLA ALLA ROMANA)

Nicola Zanghi

4 to 6 servings

This delicious light soup is easy to prepare and is a perfect preface to a heavier repast.

4 CUPS EXTRA RICH CHICKEN STOCK
1 CUP STEAMED, DICED ESCAROLE*
1 EGG, WELL BEATEN
SALT
FRESHLY GROUND BLACK PEPPER
FRESHLY GRATED PARMESAN OR
   LOCATELLI (OPTIONAL)

1. Bring the stock to a rolling boil; skim off all the fats and impurities that rise to the surface.

2. Add the escarole and return to a boil.

3. Pour the beaten egg through a colander into the soup while whisking constantly and vigorously, so the egg forms thin strands as it sets.

4. Season to taste with salt and pepper and boil for 2 minutes longer.

5. Serve the soup accompanied, if you like, by a dish of freshly grated Parmesan or *Locatelli*.

* The Florentine version of the soup is made with steamed spinach in place of the escarole.

PORK AND WATERCRESS SOUP

Gloria Bley Miller

4 servings

2 OUNCES LEAN PORK
½ BUNCH WATERCRESS
1 SCALLION
6 CUPS CHICKEN STOCK
2 SLICES FRESH GINGER
1½ TABLESPOONS MEDIUM-DRY
   SHERRY
SALT

1. Cut the pork across the grain into ¼" slices, then into ⅛" strips.

2. Remove and discard the tough watercress stems; then cut the remaining watercress into 1½" lengths.

3. Shred the scallion.

4. In a soup pot, heat the stock almost to a boil. Add the pork strips and the ginger. Reduce the heat and simmer, covered, until the meat is no longer pink, about 10 minutes.

5. Discard the slice of ginger and skim the soup if necessary. Then stir in the sherry.

6. Add the watercress and scallion shreds. Simmer, uncovered, until the watercress softens, but still retains its fresh green color, about 3 minutes.

7. Salt to taste and serve.

CABBAGE-SAUSAGE SOUP

Jane Moulton

6 to 9 servings

Sooner or later, everyone in Cleveland eats *kielbasa* (garlic-flavored Polish sausages) and stuffed cabbage; it's a Cleveland tradition. In this soup the same flavors are approximated with considerably less effort.

3 LARGE CLOVES GARLIC, PEELED
4 TABLESPOONS (½ STICK) BUTTER
  OR MARGARINE
1½ POUNDS CABBAGE, SHREDDED
  (ABOUT 3 QUARTS)
½ TO 1 POUND KIELBASA OR OTHER
  SMOKED PORK SAUSAGE, CUT INTO
  1"-LONG PIECES
2 QUARTS BEEF BROTH
5 MEDIUM-SIZED POTATOES, PEELED
  AND THINLY SLICED
¼ TEASPOON FRESHLY GROUND
  BLACK PEPPER (OPTIONAL)
SALT, TO TASTE

1. Crush the garlic on a cutting board with the flat side of a cleaver or chef's knife.

2. In a 4- to 5-quart pot, heat the butter or margarine and add the garlic.

3. When the garlic begins to sizzle, add the cabbage and stir-fry for about 3 minutes.

4. Add the sausages, broth, potatoes and pepper (if desired). Cover, bring the soup to a boil and then lower the heat and simmer for about 20 minutes, or until the potatoes are tender.

5. Before serving, taste and correct the seasoning. Raw vegetable sticks and French or Italian bread topped with melted cheese make good accompaniments.

LAMB AND LENTIL SOUP

Maria Luisa Scott and Jack Denton Scott

6 to 8 servings

We found this soup in Australia, where the lamb, grazing almost wild on vast grass-lands, had an almost gamey, but delicious flavor.

1 CUP DRIED LENTILS
1½ POUNDS LAMB SHOULDER, TRIM-
   MED OF FAT AND DICED
6 SLICES BACON, CHOPPED
3 MEDIUM-SIZED WHITE ONIONS,
   THINLY SLICED
1 SMALL TURNIP, PEELED AND DICED
1 TEASPOON SALT
½ TEASPOON BLACK PEPPER
6 CUPS BEEF BROTH

1. Rinse the lentils in cold water. Put them in a bowl and cover with fresh cold water to soak for 2 hours, then drain.

2. In a pot, cook the lamb with the bacon over medium heat until the lamb is even-ly browned.

3. Add the onions and continue cooking until they are soft.

4. Stir in the drained lentils, the turnip, salt, pepper and broth. Cover and simmer, stirring frequently, for 3 hours, or until the lamb is fork tender.

5. Taste for seasoning and serve as the Australians do with homemade bread, sweet butter and strong ale.

MATZOH BALL SOUP

Emanuel and Madeline Greenberg

4 to 6 servings

2 EGGS
1¾ TEASPOONS SALT
⅛ TEASPOON PEPPER
3 TABLESPOONS MELTED CHICKEN
   FAT
1 TABLESPOON CHOPPED PARSLEY
¾ CUP MATZOH MEAL
4 TO 6 CUPS CHICKEN STOCK

1. Beat the eggs with ¾ teaspoon of the salt, the pepper, chicken fat, parsley and ¼ cup of water.

2. Gradually stir in the matzoh meal, blending it well. Cover and refrigerate for several hours.

3. Form the matzoh mixture into balls, using about 1 tablespoon for each, and refrigerate them.

4. Into a large saucepan, bring 2½ quarts of water to a rapid boil; add the remaining teaspoon of salt. Gently lower the matzoh balls into the boiling water.

5. Reduce the heat, cover and simmer for 25 minutes. With a slotted spoon, remove the balls from the water. Keep them warm on the side.

6. Heat the chicken stock. Place the matzoh balls in the soup plates, ladle the stock over them and serve.

CALDO VERDE

Emanuel and Madeline Greenberg

8 servings

2 QUARTS WATER
2 TEASPOONS SALT
1 POUND POTATOES, PEELED AND
　DICED
1 MEDIUM-SIZED ONION, DICED
½ POUND *CHORIZO* OR PEPPERONI
　SAUSAGE, CUT INTO ¼" SLICES
4 CUPS FINELY SHREDDED KALE OR
　CABBAGE OR 2 CUPS EACH OF
　SLICED CABBAGE AND SPINACH
¼ CUP OLIVE OIL
PEPPER

1. In a large pot, bring the water to a boil. Add the salt, potatoes, onion and sausage. Boil until the potatoes are tender, about 15 to 20 minutes.

2. With a slotted spoon, remove the sausage slices from the pot and set them aside.

3. Likewise, remove the potatoes and onion from the cooking water and push them through a food mill or coarse sieve. Return the purée to the cooking water in the pot.

4. Add the kale (or substituted vegetables), olive oil and pepper to the pot. Bring to a boil and cook about 3 minutes, until the greens are just tender. Taste for salt.

5. Garnish each serving with sausage slices.

SCOTCH BROTH

Emanuel and Madeline Greenberg

6 to 8 servings

2 POUNDS LAMB SHOULDER, WITH
  BONES
¼ CUP BARLEY
2 QUARTS WATER
2 TEASPOONS SALT
SEVERAL GRINDS OF PEPPER
1 MEDIUM-SIZED ONION, CHOPPED
2 STALKS CELERY, CHOPPED

2 MEDIUM-SIZED CARROTS, DICED
½ CUP DICED WHITE TURNIP
1 LEEK (INCLUDING 2" OF THE GREEN
  PART), SLICED
1 CLOVE GARLIC, MINCED
⅛ TEASPOON THYME
⅛ TEASPOON ROSEMARY

1. Put the lamb and barley in a large pot. Add 2 quarts of water, the salt and pepper; bring to a boil. Reduce the heat, cover and simmer about 2 hours.

2. Add the vegetables, garlic and herbs. Simmer for 45 minutes longer, or until the meat and vegetables are tender.

3. Remove the meat from the pot. Trim off the fat and bones, cut the meat into small cubes and return it to the pot.

4. Skim all the fat off the soup and correct the seasoning.

5. Reheat the soup to a simmer and serve.

Note: This soup improves on standing, so if possible, make it a day or two ahead of time. After returning the lamb cubes to the pot, cover the soup and then refrigerate it. Remove the congealed fat before reheating.

HAM AND EGG SOUP

Emanuel and Madeline Greenberg

4 to 6 servings

2 CUPS CHICKEN OR BEEF STOCK
2 CUPS MILK
3 HARD-COOKED EGGS
4 TABLESPOONS (½ STICK) BUTTER
¼ POUND MUSHROOMS, SLICED
¼ CUP FLOUR
2 SLICES (ABOUT 2 OUNCES) COOKED
  HAM, FINELY CHOPPED
1 TABLESPOON CAPERS
2 TABLESPOONS LEMON JUICE
SALT, TO TASTE
PEPPER, TO TASTE

1. In a saucepan, heat the stock and milk together.

2. Separate and chop the whites and yolks of the hard-cooked eggs. Set them

aside.

3. In another saucepan, melt the butter over medium-high heat. Add the mushrooms and sauté them until lightly browned.

4. Reduce the heat, stir in the flour and cook, stirring, about 5 minutes.

5. Slowly stir in the hot stock-milk mixture and cook, stirring often, until the soup thickens.

6. Add the ham, capers and chopped egg whites. Bring the soup just to a boil. Stir in the lemon juice and taste for seasoning.

7. Serve each portion garnished with chopped egg yolks.

CHILI MEATBALL SOUP

Emanuel and Madeline Greenberg

6 servings

6 CUPS BEEF STOCK
1 BAY LEAF
3 SPRIGS PARSLEY
2 STALKS CELERY, WITH LEAVES, COARSELY CHOPPED
1 POUND GROUND CHUCK
¾ TEASPOON SALT
¾ TEASPOON CHILI POWDER, OR TO TASTE
1 SMALL ONION, GRATED
1 CUP DRY BREAD CRUMBS
⅓ CUP COOKED RICE
1 EGG, BEATEN
¼ CUP DRY SHERRY

1. Pour the stock into a large saucepan. Add the bay leaf, parsley and celery. Bring the stock to a boil, cover, and reduce the heat. Simmer for 15 minutes.

2. While the stock is simmering, prepare the meatballs. Mix together the chuck, salt, chili powder, onion, bread crumbs, rice and egg. Shape the mixture into 1'' balls.

3. Strain the stock into a large pot and bring it to a boil.

4. Add the meatballs, a few at a time, so that the stock continues to boil. Reduce the heat, cover and simmer about 20 minutes.

5. Add the sherry to the soup and simmer a few minutes longer.

6. Serve hot with corn chips as an accompaniment.

Vegetable Soups

MINESTRONE PRIMAVERA (SPRING GARDEN VEGETABLE SOUP)

Nicola Zanghi

4 to 6 servings

The staple of many Italian meals, this minestrone is also a vegetarian's delight, since the vegetable stock is water based. The soup can be varied according to whatever vegetables are at hand. Serve it with freshly grated Parmesan and toasted Italian bread, or Parmesan-toasted Italian bread.

4 TABLESPOONS (½ STICK) LIGHTLY SALTED BUTTER
½ CUP OLIVE OIL
⅓ CUP ONION, PEELED AND CUT INTO ⅓" DICE
⅔ CUP CELERY, CUT INTO ⅓" DICE
⅔ CUP CARROTS, PEELED AND CUT INTO ⅓" DICE
⅔ CUP POTATOES, PEELED AND CUT INTO ⅓" DICE
½ CUP PEELED, COARSELY CHOPPED PLUM TOMATOES

1 CUP ZUCCHINI, CUT INTO ⅓" DICE
½ CUP CANNED CHICK-PEAS*
½ CUP CANNED WHITE BEANS (CANNELINI)*
½ CUP CANNED RED KIDNEY BEANS*
SALT, TO TASTE
FRESHLY GROUND PEPPER
1 TABLESPOON CHOPPED PARSLEY
½ TEASPOON OREGANO
½ TEASPOON BASIL

1. In a 3- to 4-quart, heavy-bottomed pot, melt the butter in the oil. Add the onion and sauté over moderate heat until translucent.

2. Add the celery, carrots, potatoes, tomatoes and enough water to cover the ingredients by 2". Bring to a boil and let simmer for 45 minutes.

3. Add the zucchini and simmer 30 minutes longer.

4. Add the canned chick-peas and beans and season with salt and 8 twists of the peppermill. Stir in the herbs. Bring back to a boil, then reduce the heat and simmer for 20 minutes.

Note: The vegetables must all be cut into the same size dice for even cooking.

* Uncooked dried beans may be used in place of the canned beans. Since they swell, use ⅓ cup of each, and let them soak overnight before using. Add them to the pot with the zucchini, and skim off any impurities that might rise to the top of the soup as they simmer.

VEGETABLE SOUP WITH BASIL (SOUPE AU PISTOU)

Paula Wolfert

10 servings

I always thought *pistou* an overrated soup until I tasted this version from Marseilles. A friend from Marseilles, who gave me the recipe, told me the trick is to use a *ratatouille* as the base. The eggplant, tomatoes and green pepper should cook down until they are in a juicy, liquid state. Then, and only then, should you begin to make the soup.

½ POUND DRIED WHITE BEANS
½ POUND EGGPLANT, PEELED AND
  CUT INTO SMALL CHUNKS
SALT
¼ CUP OLIVE OIL
3 CUPS CHOPPED ONIONS
1 TABLESPOON CHOPPED GARLIC
¾ POUND SMALL, FIRM ZUCCHINI
  (ABOUT 4 OR 5), PEELED AND CUT
  INTO SMALL CHUNKS
1 MEDIUM-SIZED SWEET GREEN PEP-
  PER (OR 2 SMALL, ELONGATED
  LIGHT-GREEN ITALIAN PEPPERS),
  SEEDED, DERIBBED AND CUT INTO
  SMALL CHUNKS
2½ CUPS PEELED, SEEDED AND
  CHOPPED TOMATOES
3 QUARTS BOILING WATER
1 CUP DICED CARROTS
⅔ CUP DICED CELERY STALKS
1 CUP STRING BEANS, CUT INTO
  PIECES
1 CUP WAX BEANS, CUT INTO PIECES

BOUQUET GARNI (3 BASIL LEAVES,
  PARSLEY SPRIGS, 1 BAY LEAF AND
  2 SPRIGS FRESH THYME OR ¼ TEA-
  SPOON CRUMBLED DRIED THYME,
  TIED TOGETHER)
FRESHLY GROUND BLACK PEPPER,
  TO TASTE
¼ TEASPOON FRESHLY GRATED
  NUTMEG
1 POUND POTATOES, PEELED AND
  DICED
¾ CUP ELBOW MACARONI

Pommade:
1 CUP LARGE FRESH BASIL LEAVES,
  TORN INTO SMALL PIECES
1 TO 2 TEASPOONS FINELY CHOPPED
  GARLIC
I CUP OLIVE OIL, APPROXIMATELY
⅓ CUP GRATED PARMESAN OR
  GRUYÈRE CHEESE
SALT
FRESHLY GROUND BLACK PEPPER

1. Add enough water to the beans to cover them by 1''. Allow to soak overnight.

2. Salt the eggplant pieces and allow to drain for 15 minutes in a colander. Rinse and squeeze gently to remove the bitter juices.

3. In a deep, 8-quart capacity soup pot, heat the oil, add the onions and cook them gently, until soft. Add the garlic and cook, stirring, 2 minutes longer. Add the eggplant and cook, stirring, for 3 to 4 minutes. Add half of the zucchini and cook 3 minutes longer. Add the green pepper and cook 3 minutes longer, stirring often. Stir in the tomatoes and allow the mixture to simmer for 5 minutes, stirring often. Cover the pot and cook at a simmer for about 30 minutes.

4. Pour the boiling water into the simmering mixture, stirring briskly. Drain the white beans and add them to the pot. Cook, covered, over gentle heat for 1½ hours.

5. Add the carrots, celery, string and wax beans, *bouquet garni*, pepper and nutmeg, and continue to cook at a simmer for 20 minutes. Salt to taste.

6. Add the remaining zucchini and the potatoes and continue to cook 10 minutes longer.

Continued from preceding page

7. Stir in the macaroni and continue to cook at a simmer until the pasta is tender.

8. Meanwhile, make the *pommade*. Pound the basil leaves and garlic to a paste in a large mortar or bowl. Slowly add half of the oil, alternating with the cheese. Add the remaining olive oil, stirring until the mixture is well blended and thickened. Season with salt and pepper. Scrape into a small serving bowl or serve directly from the mortar.

9. Correct the seasoning of the soup. Serve hot and pass a bowl of freshly grated Parmesan or Gruyère cheese and the *pommade*.

MISO SOUP

Eliza and Joshua Baer

2 to 4 servings

Miso, a fermented soy bean paste, is a staple in Japanese cooking. It is usually available in health food stores and Japanese groceries. This recipe is a little more complicated, and somewhat more filling, than the *shiro miso* soups usually served as a preliminary course in Japanese restaurants.

1 TEASPOON SESAME OIL
1 TABLESPOON VEGETABLE OIL
1 RED ONION, VERY FINELY CHOPPED
1½ TEASPOONS UNBLEACHED ALL-
  PURPOSE FLOUR
4 CUPS WATER OR CHICKEN BROTH
4 TABLESPOONS LIGHT OR DARK
  MISO*
¼ CUP *MIRIN** (FORTIFIED COOKING
  SAKE), APPROXIMATELY

2 CARROTS, PEELED AND SLICED
  DIAGONALLY INTO PAPER-THIN
  OVALS
¼ CUP CHOPPED PARSLEY
SOY SAUCE, TO TASTE
1 SCALLION, SLICED DIAGONALLY
  INTO THIN OVALS

1. In a heavy saucepan, heat the sesame and vegetable oils and sauté the red onion.

2. When the onion has softened, sprinkle the flour over it to absorb the excess oils.

3. Add the water (or broth) and stir well to loosen any food sticking to the bottom of the pan. If the flour lumps, use a whisk.

4. Stirring constantly, add the *miso*. The paste will dissolve as the soup gets hotter. Bring the soup to a simmer and cook for several minutes.

5. Add ¼ cup of the *mirin*, stirring constantly.

6. Then add the carrot slices and continue simmering until the carrots are cooked to your taste, about 5 minutes for crisp carrots or 10 minutes for soft carrots.

7. Stir in the parsley, add a few dashes of soy sauce and taste the soup. If it seems somewhat bland, add additional dashes of *mirin* and soy sauce.

8. Serve the soup in individual bowls, and sprinkle each portion with sliced scallion.

Note: Using chicken broth instead of plain water will add flavor, though the chicken flavor does tend to confuse the simplicity and clarity of the soup. Vegetarians will also appreciate the strong, non-meat flavor of the basic recipe. Either way, *miso* soup has a very strengthening, almost medicinal quality, especially when served by itself. With the addition of a few more vegetables, such as shelled peas, snow peas, sliced celery, diced yellow squash or water chestnuts, the soup becomes a full meal, perfect for lunch or a late dinner. The charm of *miso* soup, however, emerges more readily when the soup is served as a first course or second course before an entrée of salmon or steamed clams.

* These ingredients are available in Japanese markets.

MUSHROOM CONSOMMÉ

Emanuel and Madeline Greenberg

6 servings

1½ POUNDS FRESH MUSHROOMS
1 TO 2 TEASPOONS LEMON JUICE
1 BUNCH SCALLIONS
2 TABLESPOONS BUTTER
1 CLOVE GARLIC, MINCED
7 CUPS BEEF OR CHICKEN STOCK
2 TABLESPOONS DRY SHERRY
SALT, TO TASTE
PEPPER, TO TASTE

1. Wipe the mushrooms with damp paper towels and, if necessary, cut away the coarse ends of the stems.

2. Remove the caps from about 6 of the mushrooms, brush them with lemon juice and set them aside for garnish.

3. In a grinder or food processor, coarsely grind the rest of the mushrooms or chop them very finely.

4. Cut off and mince the white bulbs of the scallions.

5. Mince the tender parts of green scallion tops and set them aside as a garnish.

6. In a large saucepan, heat the butter. Add the minced scallion bulbs and garlic and cook until tender, but not browned.

7. Add the ground mushrooms to the saucepan and cook for about 5 minutes, stirring occasionally.

8. Add the stock to the pan and bring it to a boil. Reduce the heat and simmer, uncovered, for about 30 minutes.

9. Cool the soup slightly, then push it firmly through a coarse sieve into a bowl so that all the liquid is extracted and some of the bits of mushroom go through the sieve.

10. Rinse or wipe out the pan and pour the soup back into it. Add the sherry and

Continued from preceding page

season with salt and pepper. Bring the soup to a boil.

11. Meanwhile, slice the reserved mushroom caps.

12. Serve when the soup is hot enough, garnishing each portion with sliced raw mushrooms and some of the minced scallion tops.

CREAM OF SAFFRON AND ALMOND SOUP

Michael Batterberry

6 to 7 servings

6 CUPS RICH CHICKEN, TURKEY OR
   DUCK BROTH, FAT REMOVED
¼ TEASPOON GROUND SAFFRON
6 OUNCES (APPROXIMATELY 1¹/₈ CUPS)
   WHOLE, BLANCHED ALMONDS
4 EGG YOLKS
1 CUP HEAVY CREAM, CHILLED
1 TEASPOON LEMON JUICE

3 DROPS OF TABASCO SAUCE
4 GRINDS OF WHITE PEPPER
SALT, TO TASTE
1 TEASPOON SALAD OIL
½ YELLOW DELICIOUS OR MACINTOSH
   APPLE, CORED
JUICE OF ½ LEMON OR LIME

1. Pour the broth into a large pot, stir in the saffron, bring to a simmer and turn off the heat. Let the broth sit for 30 minutes.

2. Reserve 12 to 14 almonds. In a blender or food processor, pulverize the rest with 1 cup of the tepid broth until you have a smooth paste.

3. Once again, bring the broth to the simmering point.

4. With a whisk, beat the egg yolks until thick. Gradually ladle a cup or so of the hot broth into the yolks, whisking constantly. Pour this mixture back into the remaining broth and continue to whisk over medium-low heat for approximately 8 minutes. The soup should only thicken to the consistency of light cream.

   Note: Do not let the mixture boil or the eggs will curdle. If an excessive cloud of steam rises from the swirling surface, remove the pan from the heat, until the steam subsides, whisking rapidly all the while. Then return it to the burner.

5. Remove the soup from the heat and stir in the heavy cream, which will halt the cooking process.

6. Whisk in the almond paste, until the soup is smooth.

7. Season with the 1 teaspoon lemon juice, the Tabasco, white pepper and salt and refrigerate.

8. Cut the reserved almonds lengthwise into thick slivers.

9. In a small, heavy frying pan, heat the oil to the smoking point. Add the almond slivers and sauté until dark golden brown, tossing them constantly with a wooden spoon. The minute the nuts turn the proper shade, quickly turn them onto paper towels, or they will scorch.

10. Finely dice the cored but unpeeled apple half. To prevent discoloration, sprin-

kle the apple generously with lemon or lime juice and mix well to coat.

11. Serve the soup in individual bowls and sprinkle each portion with some of the apple and toasted almonds.

SUMMER SQUASH SOUP

Maurice Moore-Betty

4 to 6 servings

2 MEDIUM-SIZED YELLOW SQUASH
2 SMALL ZUCCHINI
3 TABLESPOONS BUTTER
1½ CUPS PACKED FRESH CELERY
   LEAVES
6 CUPS CHICKEN STOCK
CELERY SALT
SALT
PEPPER
2 TABLESPOONS FINELY CHOPPED
   PARSLEY

1. Wash the yellow squash and zucchini and chop them, removing the seeds.

2. In a pan with a lid, melt the butter. Add the squashes and the celery leaves, cover and cook over low heat until the vegetables are tender, about 6 to 7 minutes.

3. Purée the mixture in a blender, adding a little stock to ease the blending.

4. Mix the purée with the remaining stock and correct the seasoning by adding celery salt, salt and pepper.

5. Serve the soup hot or cold, garnished with finely chopped parsley.

MULLIGATAWNY SOUP (MILGU TANNIR)

Satish Sehgal

6 servings

Though the Indian cuisine offers little in the way of soup, there is one, mulligatawny, that has become popular all over the world. It was developed by the Anglo-Indians, a class of Indians with a mixed British and Indian heritage. In Tamil, a regional Indian language, the name means "pepper water," which reflects the soup's spicy nature. This version was my favorite at Delhi's Ashoka Hotel. To get the recipe, I had to make friends with the chef, who gave it to me with great reluctance.

Continued from preceding page

6 CLOVES GARLIC, PEELED AND CHOPPED	½ TEASPOON BLACK PEPPER
ONE 1"-LONG PIECE FRESH GINGER, PEELED AND CHOPPED	2 TABLESPOONS VEGETABLE OIL
½ TEASPOON GROUND CUMIN	½ POUND GROUND BEEF
½ TEASPOON GROUND CORIANDER	4 CUPS CHICKEN BROTH
¼ TEASPOON TURMERIC	2 TABLESPOONS RICE
½ TEASPOON SALT	3 TABLESPOONS CHICK-PEA FLOUR
½ TEASPOON CAYENNE PEPPER	1 TABLESPOON LEMON JUICE
	1 TABLESPOON LIME JUICE
	6 LEMON WEDGES (OPTIONAL)

1. Put the garlic, ginger, cumin, coriander, turmeric, salt, cayenne, black pepper and 2 teaspoons of water in a blender and grind them to a smooth paste.

2. In a 4-quart pot, heat the oil over medium heat. Add the spice paste and ground beef. Stir and cook for about 15 minutes, or until the juices evaporate and the meat is well browned.

3. Add the broth to the meat and bring it to a boil.

4. Add the rice and stir.

5. In a small bowl, stir the chick-pea flour with ¼ cup of water to make a smooth paste.

6. Pour the chick-pea paste into the broth, stirring constantly. Turn the heat to high and bring the soup to a boil. Reduce the heat to low, cover the pot and let the soup simmer for 30 minutes.

7. Before serving, stir in the lemon and lime juices. Serve in individual bowls garnished with a wedge of lemon, if desired. Since the soup is fairly thick and heavy, it makes an excellent light meal, along with a salad and fruit.

CAULIFLOWER MINESTRA

Emanuel and Madeline Greenberg

4 to 6 servings

1 SMALL HEAD UNBLEMISHED CAULIFLOWER
1 TABLESPOON SALT
4 OR 5 ESCAROLE LEAVES, CUT INTO LARGE PIECES
FRESHLY GROUND BLACK PEPPER
GRATED PARMESAN
½ POUND *LINGUINE* OR SPAGHETTINI
½ CUP OLIVE OIL
¼ CUP BLANCHED, UNSALTED WHOLE ALMONDS
1 CLOVE GARLIC, CRUSHED

1. Remove and discard the leaves and stalk of the cauliflower. Wash it well and break it into flowerets.

---

2. In a large pot, bring water for the *linguine* to a boil; add 2 teaspoons of the salt.

3. Meanwhile, put the cauliflower in a large saucepan; add the escarole leaves, 2 cups of water and the remaining teaspoon of salt. Cover the pan tightly and cook 10 to 12 minutes, or until barely tender. Do not overcook. Add several grinds of pepper and 2 tablespoons grated cheese. Keep warm.

4. Add the *linguine* to the boiling, salted water. Cook according to the directions on the package until it is done, but still firm.

5. While the cauliflower and *linguine* are cooking, warm a large tureen.

6. In a heavy skillet, heat the olive oil. Add the almonds and stir until they are golden brown. Turn off the heat and add the garlic. Pour the contents of the skillet over the cooked cauliflower.

7. Drain the *linguine*, but reserve the cooking water. Place the *linguine* in the warmed tureen. Add the contents of the cauliflower pan, including all the liquid. Stir lightly.

8. Add 1 cup or more of the reserved *linguine* water, enough to make the mixture properly soupy. Serve at once with extra grated cheese.

Note: This soup takes last minute preparation and will tie up three burners on your stove as you simultaneously cook the cauliflower and the *linguine* and brown the almonds. Assemble all the ingredients in advance and plan on serving the soup 15 to 20 minutes after you start to cook the cauliflower. It makes a fine luncheon dish served with crusty bread and fruit for dessert, and it is an excellent first course before a delicate fish or chicken entrée.

FRENCH ONION SOUP

Carol Cutler

6 servings

The fame of French onion soup can be attributed to the late lamented produce area of Paris known as *Les Halles*, which came to life in the wee hours of the morning. The area took on a throbbing, boisterous, aromatic life of its own and late night revelers would descend upon its all-night restaurants for a revivifying jolt of the steamy hot broth. *Les Halles* may have changed its character and location, but *soupe à l'oignon* will remain a delicious classic forever.

4 TABLESPOONS (½ STICK) BUTTER
1 TABLESPOON OIL
6 MEDIUM-SIZED ONIONS, THINLY
    SLICED
½ TEASPOON PREPARED FRENCH
    MUSTARD
1 TEASPOON SALT

PEPPER, TO TASTE
1 TEASPOON FLOUR
1 TEASPOON BEEF EXTRACT
1 CUP DRY WHITE WINE
2½ CUPS BEEF STOCK
¼ CUP GRATED GRUYÈRE
6 SLICES FRENCH BREAD, TOASTED

1. In a heavy pot, heat the butter and oil. Add the onions, mustard, salt and pep-

Continued from preceding page

per. Cook the onions over very low heat until they turn a dark brown and have reduced greatly in bulk, about 30 minutes.

Note: The long, slow cooking is very important to give the onions a mild, sweet flavor.

2. Stir in the flour and beef extract and mix well.

3. While continuing to stir, slowly pour in the wine and stock. Slowly bring to a boil and simmer for 15 minutes.

4. Pile the grated cheese on the toast slices and slip them under the broiler for 30 seconds or so, until the cheese melts and browns a little.

5. Ladle the soup into individual soup bowls and place a slice of the cheese-toast on top.

Note: By increasing the size and number of the cheese-toasts, *soupe à l'oignon* can become a main course at either lunch or supper, accompanied by a chilled white wine, such as Muscadet or California Chablis, and followed by salad and dessert.

IOWA CORN CHOWDER

Emanuel and Madeline Greenberg

6 to 8 servings

ONE 1½" CUBE OF SALT PORK, FINELY CHOPPED
1 SMALL ONION, CHOPPED
½ GREEN PEPPER, DICED
1 SMALL STALK CELERY, CHOPPED
2 CUPS WATER
4 MEDIUM-SIZED POTATOES, PEELED AND DICED
SALT

2 CUPS MILK
2 CUPS LIGHT CREAM OR HALF-AND-HALF
2 CUPS FRESH CORN KERNELS (ABOUT 6 LARGE EARS OF CORN), OR 2 CUPS FROZEN CORN KERNELS
PINCH OF NUTMEG
WHITE PEPPER, TO TASTE

1. In a large pot, heat the salt pork until the fat is rendered and the scraps are brown and crisp. Lift out the cracklings and set them aside to drain on paper towels.

2. Add the onion, green pepper and celery to the pot; cook until they are softened.

3. Then add 2 cups of water, the potatoes and 1 teaspoon of salt. Bring the mixture to a boil, cover the pot and cook until the potatoes are tender, about 12 to 15 minutes.

4. Add the milk, cream and corn to the pot. Reduce the heat and bring the soup to a simmer, uncovered. Cook about 10 minutes, or just until the corn kernels are tender. Do not allow it to boil.

5. Add the nutmeg, pepper and additional salt to taste.

6. Serve in individual bowls and garnish each serving with a few browned pork bits.

POTATO SOUP PARMESAN

Florence Fabricant

6 servings

2 TABLESPOONS OLIVE OIL
½ CUP CHOPPED ONION
1 LARGE CLOVE GARLIC, CRUSHED
1½ CUPS VERY FINELY CHOPPED,
    PEELED POTATOES (ABOUT 2 LARGE
    POTATOES)
2 CUPS WATER

1½ CUPS GRATED PARMESAN
2 CUPS MILK
2 TO 3 TEASPOONS SALT
FRESHLY GROUND WHITE PEPPER
½ CUP CREAM
1 TABLESPOON FINELY MINCED
    PARSLEY

1. In a heavy saucepan, heat the oil, add the onion and sauté until it is soft but not brown.

2. Add the garlic and potatoes and stir for a moment. Then add the water, bring to a boil and simmer, covered, for 20 minutes.

3. Stir in 1 cup of the cheese.

4. Purée the soup in a blender or food processor until fairly smooth. Return it to the saucepan.

5. Add the milk and season to taste with salt and pepper. Heat for 5 minutes, then remove from the heat and stir in the cream.

6. Sprinkle each serving with parsley and Parmesan.

GREEN PEA SOUP

Rona Deme

6 to 8 servings

In England, when this soup is very thick it is known as pease pudding.

1 HAM BONE
2 POUNDS SPLIT GREEN PEAS
1 ONION
2 STALKS CELERY
2 CARROTS
GRATED CHEDDAR CHEESE (OPTIONAL)
SOUR CREAM (OPTIONAL)

1. Place the ham bone in a large pot and cover it with 4 quarts of water. Bring the water to a boil.

2. Add the dried peas, onion, celery and carrots. Stir and then simmer for 2 hours.

3. Remove the ham bone and purée the soup through a food mill or chinois.

4. Return the soup to the pot and reheat it before serving. If it is too thick, add a little water until it reaches the desired consistency.

Continued from preceding page

5. Serve each portion with a little grated cheddar cheese and a dab of sour cream, if desired. In England, it is also customary to have malt vinegar on the table for additional seasoning.

CREAM OF CARROT SOUP
(CRÈME CRECY À L'ORANGE)

Emanuel and Madeline Greenberg

6 servings

3 TABLESPOONS BUTTER
1 MEDIUM-SIZED ONION, CHOPPED
1 POUND CARROTS, SCRAPED AND
  THINLY SLICED
2 CUPS WATER
1½ TO 2 CUPS ORANGE JUICE
1½ TEASPOONS FRESH OR ½ TEA-
  SPOON DRIED TARRAGON
SALT, TO TASTE
PEPPER, TO TASTE
1 TO 1½ CUPS LIGHT CREAM
2 TABLESPOONS SLIVERED, TOASTED
  ALMONDS

1. In a large saucepan, heat the butter. Add the onion and cook until it has softened.

2. Add the carrots, water, 1½ cups of orange juice, tarragon, salt and pepper to the saucepan. Cover and bring to a boil. Reduce the heat and simmer about 30 minutes, or until the carrots are very tender.

3. Cool the mixture slightly; purée 2 cups at a time in a blender until very smooth. If the purée is too thick, add more orange juice.

4. Refrigerate until very cold. Before serving, stir in 1 cup of cream. If the soup seems too thick, stir in a little more cream. Taste for seasoning.

5. Serve the soup in chilled bowls garnished with the almonds.

INDIAN SPLIT PEA SOUP

Satish Sehgal

6 servings

Since this soup contains no fats or meats, it is very light and easily digestible. When we were young, my mother used to make this soup whenever somebody in the family was sick. When well-spiced, it is a very good soup for any occasion.

1 CUP YELLOW SPLIT PEAS
5 CUPS CHICKEN BROTH
20 BLACK PEPPERCORNS
15 CLOVES
½ TEASPOON GROUND TURMERIC
½ TEASPOON SALT
6 LEMON WEDGES

1. Put the split peas and broth in a stockpot and bring to a boil. Skim off any foam that rises to the surface.

2. Add the peppercorns, cloves, turmeric and salt. Cover the pot and simmer on low heat for about 1½ hours, or until the peas are absolutely tender. Remove from the heat and let the soup cool a bit.

3. In a blender or food processor, purée the soup until it is very smooth and return it to the pot.

4. Reheat the soup by bringing it to a boil; if it is too thick, add some hot water.

5. Serve in individual bowls garnished with a lemon wedge.

COACH HOUSE BLACK BEAN SOUP

Emanuel and Madeline Greenberg

8 servings

1 POUND DRIED BLACK BEANS
2½ QUARTS CHICKEN OR BEEF STOCK, WATER OR A MIXTURE OF STOCK AND WATER
4 TABLESPOONS (½ STICK) BUTTER
2 STALKS CELERY, FINELY CHOPPED
2 MEDIUM-SIZED ONIONS, FINELY CHOPPED
1½ TABLESPOONS FLOUR
¼ CUP FINELY CHOPPED PARSLEY
1 LARGE LEEK, FINELY SLICED
1 CLOVE GARLIC, CRUSHED
1 BAY LEAF
BONE AND RIND OF A COOKED SMOKED HAM
1½ TEASPOONS SALT
¼ TEASPOON FRESHLY GROUND PEPPER
½ CUP MADEIRA
1 HARD-COOKED EGG, FINELY CHOPPED
LEMON SLICES

1. Wash the beans. Cover them with cold water and let them soak overnight.

2. Drain the beans and place them in a large pot. Add the stock, water or stock mixture. Bring to a boil, cover, reduce the heat and simmer for 1½ hours.

3. In another large pot, heat the butter. Add the celery and onions and sauté until they are softened, but not brown, about 8 to 10 minutes.

4. Stir in the flour and parsley and cook, stirring constantly, about 1 minute.

5. Stir in the beans and their liquid. Add the leek, garlic, bay leaf, ham bone and rind, salt and pepper. Cover and simmer over low heat about 4 hours. Check occasionally and add a little water if the soup seems to be getting too thick.

Continued from preceding page

6. Remove and discard the ham bone, rind and bay leaf. Put the soup through a strainer, pressing hard to extract all of the liquid, and return it to the pot.

7. Add the Madeira and reheat the soup. Taste and correct the seasoning. Stir in the chopped egg and serve. Garnish each portion with a lemon slice.

CABBAGE, CHESTNUT AND BEAN SOUP

Elizabeth Schneider Colchie

6 servings

¾ TO 1 POUND CHESTNUTS*
3 QUARTS STRONG MEAT STOCK
1 CUP DRIED PINTO BEANS, HALF COOKED
1 LEEK, SLICED
2 POUNDS CABBAGE, CORED AND SLICED
¼ POUND SLAB BACON, RIND REMOVED AND CUT INTO ½" DICE

1 LARGE CLOVE GARLIC, PEELED AND MASHED
2 LARGE WHITE TURNIPS, PEELED AND QUARTERED
4 MEDIUM-SIZED CARROTS, PEELED AND QUARTERED
1 TEASPOON THYME
SALT

1. Preheat the oven to 450 F.

2. Cut one or two slits in each chestnut, extending all the way from the base to the tip on one side. Place the chestnuts in a cake pan with ⅓ cup of water and bake in the preheated oven for 10 minutes; shake the pan and bake for 5 more minutes.

3. Turn off the oven. Take out 5 or 6 nuts at a time and peel and remove their shells.

4. In a large, heavy soup pot, combine the chestnuts with the remaining ingredients, except the salt, and simmer, partly covered, for about 2 hours.

5. Add salt to taste. Cool and refrigerate (to allow the flavor to develop). Reheat to serve.

* Or use about 1 cup of dried chestnuts, soaked.

HOT BORSCHT

Emanuel and Madeline Greenberg

6 servings

The Russian Tea Room of New York offers this version of the traditional Russian soup.

4 CUPS BEEF STOCK
3 LARGE BEETS, PEELED AND FINELY
   CHOPPED
2 ONIONS, PEELED AND FINELY
   CHOPPED
2 STALKS CELERY, FINELY CHOPPED
1 PARSNIP, PEELED AND FINELY
   CHOPPED
1 CARROT, PEELED AND FINELY
   CHOPPED

1 CUP COARSELY SHREDDED CABBAGE
1 CAN (8 OUNCES) TOMATO PURÉE
1 TEASPOON SUGAR
1 CLOVE GARLIC, SPLIT
SALT, TO TASTE
PEPPER, TO TASTE
½ CUP SOUR CREAM
FRESH DILL, FINELY CHOPPED

1. In a large pot, bring the stock to a boil. Add the beets, onions, celery, parsnip and carrot. Return to a boil; cover, reduce the heat and simmer for 20 minutes.

2. Add the cabbage, tomato purée, sugar and garlic. Simmer until the cabbage is just tender, about 15 minutes.

3. Taste for seasoning, adding salt and pepper as necessary.

4. Ladle the borscht into soup bowls and garnish each serving with sour cream and a sprinkling of chopped dill.

TANGY TOMATO BISQUE

Emanuel and Madeline Greenberg

6 servings

1½ TABLESPOONS BUTTER
2 MEDIUM-SIZED ONIONS, CHOPPED
   (ABOUT 1 CUP)
1 CLOVE GARLIC, MINCED
1 CAN (20 TO 30 OUNCES) WHOLE
   TOMATOES, UNDRAINED
2 CUPS CHICKEN STOCK

¼ CUP RICE
SALT, TO TASTE
PEPPER, TO TASTE
¼ TEASPOON DRIED BASIL
⅛ TEASPOON DRIED THYME
2 TO 2½ CUPS HALF-AND-HALF
DASH OF TABASCO SAUCE (OPTIONAL)

1. In a large saucepan, heat the butter; add the onions and garlic. Cook until tender, but not browned.

2. Add the undrained tomatoes, stock, rice, salt, pepper, basil and thyme. Cover partially and bring the mixture to a boil. Reduce the heat and simmer about 45 minutes.

3. Cool the soup slightly, then put it through a food mill, extracting as much of the solids as possible. If a smoother texture is desired, whirl the mixture in a blender, about 2 cups at a time.

4. Rinse or wipe out the soup pot and pour the puréed soup back into it. Stir in 2 cups of the half-and-half, or enough to thin the soup to the desired consistency. Taste for seasoning and add a dash of Tabasco, if desired.

5. Heat the soup just to a boil and serve immediately.

KAPLAN'S MUSHROOM-BARLEY SOUP

Emanuel and Madeline Greenberg

Emanuel and Madeline Greenberg

6 to 8 servings

Kaplan's in the Delmonico Hotel in Manhattan is one of the last strongholds of authentic "deli" food, which includes this soup.

12 DRIED MUSHROOMS
2 QUARTS WATER PLUS WATER FOR
  SOAKING THE MUSHROOMS
¼ CUP BARLEY
2 MEDIUM-SIZED POTATOES, PEELED
  AND DICED
2 CARROTS, SCRAPED AND DICED

2 TEASPOONS SALT
SEVERAL GRINDS OF PEPPER
2 TABLESPOONS OIL
2 MEDIUM-SIZED ONIONS, DICED
2 TABLESPOONS FLOUR
1 CUP CHICKEN STOCK

1. Rinse the mushrooms. Cover them with cold water and let them stand about 10 minutes; drain and finely slice them.

2. In a large pot, combine 2 quarts of water, the mushrooms, barley, potatoes, carrots, salt and pepper. Bring to a boil. Cover, reduce the heat and simmer for 1 hour.

3. Meanwhile, heat the oil in a skillet. Add the onions and sauté until they are golden brown. Add them to the soup after it has simmered for an hour; then simmer for another 30 minutes.

4. Stir the flour gradually into the chicken stock, stirring constantly, until smooth. Add the flour-and-stock mixture to the soup and simmer 15 minutes longer, stirring occasionally. Taste and correct the seasoning.

MAINE CREAM OF POTATO SOUP

Emanuel and Madeline Greenberg

8 servings

6 TABLESPOONS (¾ STICK) BUTTER
4 MEDIUM-SIZED ONIONS, THINLY
  DICED
4 STALKS CELERY, FINELY CHOPPED
2 POUNDS POTATOES, PEELED AND
  DICED
BOILING WATER
SALT
PEPPER
2 QUARTS MILK
2 TABLESPOONS FLOUR
PAPRIKA

1. In a 2½-quart pot, heat 4 tablespoons of the butter. Add the onions and celery and cook them until softened.

2. Add the potatoes, stir well and cook for a few minutes longer.

3. Add enough boiling water to cover the vegetables; then add 2 teaspoons of salt and $1/_8$ teaspoon of pepper. Cover and simmer until the potatoes are tender, about 15 to 20 minutes.

4. Add the milk and simmer until almost boiling.

5. Blend the flour with the remaining 2 tablespoons of butter. Stir the mixture into the soup, bit by bit; cook, stirring often, until the soup is slightly thickened. Taste it for seasoning and add more salt and pepper, if necessary.

6. Serve and sprinkle each portion of soup with a little paprika.

GEORGIA PEANUT SOUP

Emanuel and Madeline Greenberg

6 servings

It should come as no surprise that peanut soup is becoming more popular—especially around Washington, D.C.

2 TABLESPOONS BUTTER
1 STALK CELERY, FINELY CHOPPED
1 MEDIUM-SIZED ONION, FINELY
   CHOPPED
1 TABLESPOON FLOUR
4 CUPS CHICKEN STOCK
½ CUP CHUNK-STYLE PEANUT BUTTER
1½ CUPS HALF-AND-HALF OR MILK
SALT
PEPPER
¼ CUP CHOPPED PEANUTS
PAPRIKA

1. In a large saucepan, melt the butter over low heat. Add the celery and onion and sauté them until softened, but not browned.

2. Stir in the flour and cook for 2 or 3 minutes. Gradually stir in the chicken stock and bring to a boil.

3. Blend in the peanut butter and simmer about 15 minutes, stirring occasionally.

4. Add the half-and-half (or milk) to the pan and heat the soup just to the boiling point. Taste for seasoning and add salt and pepper, if necessary.

5. Garnish each portion of soup with chopped peanuts and a light sprinkling of paprika.

Note: They may not do it in Georgia, but a bit of curry powder makes a nice addition to this soup. If you want to try it, add $1/_8$ teaspoon or more, along with the flour.

Savory and Sweet Cold Soups

CURRIED FRUIT SOUP

Carol Cutler

8 servings

2 CUPS CHICKEN STOCK
2 APPLES, PEELED, CORED AND CUT
INTO CHUNKS (PREFERABLY
MACINTOSH OR STAYMAN)
1 POUND BANANAS, PEELED AND CUT
INTO CHUNKS
1 POTATO, PEELED AND CUT INTO
CHUNKS

1 SMALL ONION, PEELED AND CUT
INTO CHUNKS
2 TO 3 TEASPOONS CURRY POWDER
1 PINT LIGHT CREAM
1 APPLE, GRATED AND TOSSED WITH
LEMON JUICE (OPTIONAL)
GRATED LEMON RIND (OPTIONAL)

1. In a 1½- to 2-quart saucepan, heat the chicken stock. Add the apples, bananas, potato and onion. Cover and simmer until the fruits and vegetables are soft, about 15 minutes.

2. Spoon the cooked fruits and vegetables into a blender with the stock. Add the curry (the exact amount will depend on your taste for curry, and the fact that the coldness of the soup will diminish the intensity of the seasonings). Purée the mixture until smooth and pour it into a large bowl.

3. Stir in the cream and chill.

4. Garnish each portion with either the grated apple or lemon rind, as desired.

VICHYSSOISE

Emanuel and Madeline Greenberg

8 servings

As every gourmet knows, vichyssoise was originally created by the great French chef Louis Diat when he reigned in the kitchens of the old Ritz-Carlton Hotel in New York City. Actually, he took the leek and potato soup of his childhood, dressed it up, chilled it and named it for a famous spa that was close to his native village in France.

2 TABLESPOONS BUTTER
4 LEEKS, THINLY SLICED (WHITE
    PART ONLY)
1 MEDIUM-SIZED ONION, CHOPPED
5 MEDIUM-SIZED POTATOES, PEELED
    AND SLICED
4 CUPS WATER OR CHICKEN STOCK
2 TEASPOONS SALT
$1/_8$ TEASPOON WHITE PEPPER
2 CUPS HALF-AND-HALF
2 CUPS HEAVY CREAM
CHOPPED CHIVES

1. In a large pot, melt the butter. Add the leeks and onion and sauté until they are softened, but not browned.

2. Add the potatoes, water (or stock), salt and pepper to the pot. Cover and bring to a boil. Reduce the heat and simmer about 30 minutes, or until the potatoes are very soft.

3. Cool the soup slightly, then, 2 cups at a time, purée it in a blender until smooth.

4. Return the soup to the heat, add the half-and-half and bring it to a boil. Then strain the soup into a bowl.

5. Refrigerate the soup until it is very cold.

6. Before serving, taste and correct the seasoning and stir in the heavy cream. Garnish each portion with chopped chives.

Note: For a variation known as vichyssoise à la Ritz, add 1 part chilled tomato juice to 3 parts of the above soup.

CHAMPAGNE FRUIT SOUP

Emanuel and Madeline Greenberg

8 servings

1 CAN (16 OUNCES) PITTED DARK
    SWEET CHERRIES
1 CAN (16 OUNCES) PITTED SOUR
    RED CHERRIES
2 TABLESPOONS SUGAR
1 TEASPOON GRATED ORANGE RIND
½ TEASPOON CINNAMON

PINCH OF SALT
2 TABLESPOONS CORNSTARCH
⅓ CUP ORANGE LIQUEUR
3 SEEDLESS ORANGES
1 TART APPLE, PEELED AND COARSELY
    GRATED
1 BOTTLE CHILLED CHAMPAGNE

1. Into a saucepan, pour the sweet and sour cherries with their juices. Add the sugar, orange rind, cinnamon and salt, and stir in the cornstarch.

2. Cook over medium heat, stirring often, until the mixture thickens and comes to a boil.

3. Stir in the orange liqueur and transfer the mixture to a bowl. Cool slightly.

Continued from preceding page

4. Peel the oranges and section them into the bowl of soup so that all the juices are caught. Add the apple. Chill very well.

5. To serve, ladle the soup into chilled bowls and add a generous splash of champagne—2 to 3 ounces—to each portion.

Note: A good California or New York State extra-dry champagne is fine for this soup. If you like, serve each guest a split (6½-ounce bottle) of chilled champagne —some to be added to the soup, the rest to be drunk with the meal.

GAZPACHO JEREZ

Emanuel and Madeline Greenberg

6 servings

There are many delicious *gazpachos*, but in our experience this is the best. The special ingredient in it is sherry vinegar, although plain red wine vinegar is good, too.

5 MEDIUM-SIZED RIPE TOMATOES (ABOUT 1½ POUNDS), PEELED
½ CUP CHOPPED ONION
1 CUCUMBER, PEELED AND CUBED
½ GREEN PEPPER, SEEDED, DE-RIBBED AND CUT INTO LARGE PIECES
2 CLOVES GARLIC, QUARTERED
¼ CUP OLIVE OIL
2 TABLESPOONS SHERRY VINEGAR OR RED WINE VINEGAR
½ CUP TOMATO JUICE, APPROXIMATELY
½ CUP CRUSHED ICE, APPROXIMATELY

SALT, TO TASTE
PEPPER, TO TASTE
DASH OF TABASCO SAUCE

Garnishes:
3 SLICES FIRM WHITE BREAD
4 TABLESPOONS (½ STICK) BUTTER OR ¼ CUP OLIVE OIL
1 CLOVE GARLIC, PARTIALLY SPLIT
½ CUP FINELY CHOPPED GREEN PEPPER
½ CUP FINELY CHOPPED ONION
½ CUP FINELY CHOPPED CUCUMBER
½ CUP PEELED, FINELY CHOPPED TOMATOES

1. Place a strainer over a large bowl. Halve and seed the tomatoes over the strainer so that the seeds are caught and the juices fall into the bowl. Push any bits of pulp through the strainer, then remove the strainer and discard the seeds.

2. Cut the seeded tomato halves into chunks and place them in the bowl. Add the remaining vegetables, garlic, olive oil and vinegar.

3. Whirl the tomato mixture in a blender, 2 cups at a time, until it is finely chopped, but not liquefied.

4. After blending, pour the *gazpacho* into a large bowl and stir in equal parts of tomato juice and crushed ice, a tablespoon at a time; do not make the mixture too liquid. Season with salt, pepper and Tabasco.

5. Refrigerate the soup for several hours, or until it is very cold. Stir well, taste

and correct the seasoning.

6. Meanwhile, prepare the croutons. Trim the crusts off the bread and cut it into ½'' cubes.

7. In a skillet, heat the butter (or olive oil) with the garlic clove.

8. Add the bread cubes and fry, stirring often, until they are crisp and golden brown.

9. Drain the croutons on paper towels.

10. Ladle the *gazpacho* into chilled bowls and set out small bowls containing the croutons and the rest of the garnishes. Use some or all of the garnishes, as desired.

COLD CREAM OF SORREL SOUP

Paul Rubinstein

6 servings

1 POUND FRESH SORREL LEAVES OR
  1 JAR (1 POUND) PRESERVED SORREL
5 CUPS CHICKEN BROTH OR BOUILLON
1 CUP HEAVY CREAM
1 CUP SOUR CREAM
½ TEASPOON SALT
¼ TEASPOON FRESHLY GROUND
  WHITE PEPPER
2 TABLESPOONS MAGGI LIQUID SEA-
  SONING
3 HARD-COOKED EGGS

1. If you are using fresh sorrel, cut away any thick stems, then wash, drain and finely chop the leaves. If you are using preserved sorrel, simply drain it.

2. In a saucepan, bring the chicken broth and sorrel to a simmer; cook, covered, for 15 minutes over medium-low heat. Remove from the heat and allow the soup to cool.

3. With a whisk, beat in the heavy cream and then the sour cream, until the soup is smooth.

4. Stir in the salt, pepper and Maggi and refrigerate.

5. Peel the hard-cooked eggs and cut them in half lengthwise.

6. Serve the soup cold, with half an egg floating in each portion.

CHLODNIK (COLD CUCUMBER AND BUTTERMILK SOUP)

Emanuel and Madeline Greenberg

6 to 8 servings

Bulgarians, Poles and Russians dote on this frosty soup made with summer's fresh cucumbers.

4 CUPS BUTTERMILK
2 CUPS SOUR CREAM
1 CUP CHOPPED, COOKED SHRIMP, VEAL OR CHICKEN
1 LARGE CUCUMBER, PEELED, SEEDED AND DICED
½ CUP CHOPPED SCALLIONS (INCLUDING SOME OF THE GREEN PART)

2 TABLESPOONS CHOPPED FRESH DILL
2 TABLESPOONS CHOPPED FRESH FENNEL OR ½ TEASPOON GROUND FENNEL SEEDS
1 CLOVE GARLIC, CRUSHED
SALT
PEPPER
2 HARD-COOKED EGGS, CHOPPED

1. In a large bowl, beat together the buttermilk and sour cream until smooth.

2. Add the shrimp (or meat), vegetables, herbs and seasonings; stir gently but thoroughly. Refrigerate the soup for several hours, or until it is very cold.

3. Before serving, stir the soup, add salt and pepper and correct for seasoning. Garnish each portion with a little of the chopped egg.

COLD BORSCHT

Emanuel and Madeline Greenberg

6 servings

2 MEDIUM-SIZED ONIONS, FINELY CHOPPED
2 SMALL CARROTS, SCRAPED AND FINELY CHOPPED
2 SPRIGS PARSLEY
6 CUPS WATER
4 LARGE BEETS, PEELED AND COARSELY SHREDDED
1 TEASPOON SALT, OR TO TASTE

1 TEASPOON SUGAR, OR TO TASTE
SEVERAL GRINDS OF PEPPER
JUICE OF 1 LEMON
1 SMALL CAN (8 OUNCES) DICED BEETS, CHILLED
½ CUCUMBER, PEELED, SEEDED AND FINELY CHOPPED
1 CUP SOUR CREAM, APPROXIMATELY

1. In a large pot, combine the onions, carrots, parsley and 6 cups of water. Bring to a boil and cook for 15 minutes.

2. Add the beets and cook about 15 minutes more, or until they are tender.

3. Strain the mixture into a bowl while hot, pressing the vegetables to extract all of their liquids. Add the salt, sugar, pepper and lemon juice. Stir well and adjust the seasoning to taste.

4. Refrigerate the soup until it is very cold.

5. Before serving, stir in the can of beets, with their liquid, and the chopped cucumber. Taste for seasoning.

6. Ladle the soup into bowls and top with a generous spoonful of sour cream.

CHILLED FRESH TOMATO SOUP

Emanuel and Madeline Greenberg

6 to 8 servings

2 TO 2½ POUNDS RIPE TOMATOES
¼ CUP GRATED ONION
1 TEASPOON SALT
¼ TEASPOON PEPPER
½ TEASPOON DRIED THYME, FINELY
   CRUMBLED
¼ CUP MAYONNAISE
1 TABLESPOON WINE VINEGAR
¾ TEASPOON CURRY POWDER, OR
   TO TASTE
3 TABLESPOONS MINCED FRESH
   CORIANDER*

1. Dip the tomatoes first in boiling water and then in cold water. Slip off the skins.

2. Place a strainer over a bowl. Halve the tomatoes and remove the seeds over the strainer so that the juices fall into the bowl. Push any bits of pulp connected to the seeds through the strainer into the bowl. Remove the strainer, cut the tomatoes into chunks and add them to the bowl.

3. In small batches, put the tomatoes and their juices in the jar of a blender and whirl briefly so they are finely chopped but not liquefied.

4. When all the tomatoes are chopped, combine them in a large bowl with the onion, salt, pepper and thyme. Chill the soup until very cold.

5. Meanwhile, combine the mayonnaise with the vinegar, curry powder and fresh coriander. Ladle the soup into chilled bowls and top each portion with a spoonful of the seasoned mayonnaise.

6. Before serving, stir the soup well and correct the seasoning.

* Also called *cilantro* or Chinese parsley

TIGER'S TAIL

Emanuel and Madeline Greenberg

4 to 6 servings

2 TABLESPOONS BUTTER
2 TABLESPOONS ONION, FINELY
   CHOPPED
2 TEASPOONS CURRY POWDER, OR
   TO TASTE
1 TABLESPOON FLOUR
3½ CUPS CHICKEN STOCK
¼ CUP DRY SHERRY
2 EGG YOLKS, LIGHTLY BEATEN
½ CUP CREAM
⅓ CUP FINELY DICED, TART, UN-
   PEELED RED-SKINNED APPLE

1. In a large pot, heat the butter. Add the onion and curry powder. Saute about 5 minutes, or until the onion is softened. Stir in the flour, mixing it well; cook for a few minutes.

2. Slowly stir in the chicken stock, then the sherry. Bring to a boil, stirring constantly.

3. Gradually stir some of the hot soup into the egg yolks, then stir the yolks into the soup pot. Reduce the heat to low. Cook, stirring, about 1 minute, or until slightly thickened.

4. Strain the soup into a bowl; cover and cool slightly. Refrigerate until it is very cold.

5. Just before serving, stir in the cream and taste for seasoning. Serve the soup in chilled bowls and garnish it with the chopped apple.

JADE AND RUBIES

Emanuel and Madeline Greenberg

6 servings

3 MEDIUM-SIZED, FULLY RIPE
   AVOCADOS
3 TABLESPOONS LEMON JUICE
1 LARGE CUCUMBER
3 CUPS CHICKEN STOCK
¾ CUP SOUR CREAM
1½ TEASPOONS SALT, OR TO TASTE
DASH OF TABASCO SAUCE
3 TOMATOES, PEELED AND DICED

1. Peel and cube the avocados. Toss them with the lemon juice.

2. Peel, seed and cube the cucumber. Put half of the avocado and cucumber in the jar of a blender with half of the stock. Blend until smooth and pour the mixture into a bowl. Repeat with the remaining avocado, cucumber and stock.

3. Beat the sour cream, salt and Tabasco into the soup. Refrigerate until very cold.

4. Before serving, stir the soup and taste for seasoning. Ladle it into chilled bowls and garnish each portion with diced tomato.

MAXWELL'S PLUM COLD MELON SOUP

Emanuel and Madeline Greenberg

4 servings

Daniel Fuchs created this unusual melon soup for New York's Maxwell's Plum restaurant.

1 LARGE, RIPE HONEYDEW MELON
JUICE OF 2 LEMONS, STRAINED
2 TEASPOONS CHOPPED FRESH MINT,
   PLUS 4 MINT SPRIGS
PINCH OF CINNAMON
¼ CUP YOGURT, APPROXIMATELY
⅓ CUP LIGHT CREAM

1. Cut the melon in half. Discard the seeds and remove the rind. Cut the melon into chunks and put them in a bowl together with the lemon juice.

2. In a blender, purée half of the melon chunks and lemon juice and pour the mixture into a bowl; repeat with the second half. Stir in the chopped mint and cinnamon. Cover and refrigerate the soup until it is thoroughly chilled.

3. Before serving, stir in ¼ cup of the yogurt and the cream. Taste for seasoning and add more lemon juice, if desired. If the soup seems too thick, thin it with extra yogurt.

4. Serve the soup in chilled bowls and garnish it with mint sprigs.

JERSEY BLUEBERRY SOUP

Emanuel and Madeline Greenberg

6 servings

People in New Jersey love their blueberries and find lots of ways to enjoy them, including soup. This version is served at New York's Pen & Pencil Restaurant.

1 PINT BLUEBERRIES
2 CUPS WATER
½ CUP SUGAR, OR TO TASTE
ONE 3" STICK CINNAMON
RIND AND JUICE OF 1 LEMON
½ CUP FRUITY WHITE WINE
2 CUPS SOUR CREAM

1. Rinse and drain the blueberries, then put them in a large pot. Add the water, sugar, cinnamon, lemon rind and lemon juice.

2. Bring the soup to a boil, then reduce the heat and simmer, uncovered, for 15 minutes. Remove the cinnamon stick and strain, if desired. Taste for sweetness.

3. Refrigerate the soup until it is very cold.

4. Before serving, stir in the wine and then beat in the sour cream.

APPLECOT COOLER

Emanuel and Madeline Greenberg

6 to 8 servings

½ CUP DRIED APRICOTS
½ CUP BOILING WATER
1 CAN (12 OUNCES) APRICOT NECTAR
2 CUPS APPLE JUICE
½ CUP YOGURT
¾ CUP CRUSHED ICE

1. Place the apricots in a small bowl, cover them with the boiling water, and let them stand for 5 minutes, then drain.

2. Transfer the drained apricots to the jar of a blender. Add ½ cup of the apricot nectar and purée the mixture.

3. Add the remaining apricot nectar, apple juice and yogurt to the jar and whirl until smooth. Pour the soup into a bowl and refrigerate until very cold.

4. Just before serving, stir in the crushed ice. Ladle the soup into tall glasses.

Note: If the jar of your blender is on the small side, blend the apricot purée with only half of the additional liquids and pour the mixture into a bowl. Then whirl the remaining liquids in the blender until they are very well combined, add them to the first batch and mix thoroughly.